SO-DZH-706

DISCARDED

PORTRAITS

OF

POWER

D
412.6
G7
1969

PORTRAITS

OF

POWER

972534

By

Norman D. Greenwald

Introduction by

Louis M. Lyons

LTL ĽAMAR TECH ĽIBRARY

Edited by

Richard E. Myers

Biography Index Reprint Series

 BOOKS FOR LIBRARIES PRESS
FREEPORT, NEW YORK

© Copyright 1961 by Berkshire Publishing Company, Inc.

Reprinted 1969 by arrangement

To my Mother

STANDARD BOOK NUMBER:

8369-8001-8

LIBRARY OF CONGRESS CATALOG CARD NUMBER:

73-101828

PRINTED IN THE UNITED STATES OF AMERICA

CONTENTS

Thomas Carlyle has observed that "biography is the only true history." In this age of centralized government, push-button warfare, and impersonalized society, the ultimate responsibility for the well-being and security of us all frequently falls on one powerful man. The success or failure of modern government is often measured by the virtues and the faults of the man in power.

A biographical method is used in this book to introduce the contrasting political institutions and problems of twelve important foreign nations. The particular selection of the men here may seem quite arbitrary. In general, however, the author has drawn portraits of representative leaders of liberal, totalitarian, developed and under-developed nations.

This study is based on lectures delivered in the summer of 1960 over New England's great educational radio and television station WGBH Boston. The author is greatly indebted to the overworked, but ever-cheerful staff and crew of WGBH for much encouragement and assistance. Special thanks go to Miss Barbara Federer who helped draft and proofread this manuscript, and to Richard Myers, who edited it.

NORMAN GREENWALD

Northeastern University

INTRODUCTION

The lives of the twelve national leaders here traced suggest the convulsive political changes of our times. The paths to power in these portraits follow no single pattern. But all have shown the quality of leadership in crisis: indeed crisis is the single common denominator of their lives and of their times. Some led their people to independence, some to revolutionary social change, others to counter-revolution. All have ridden the whirlwind and shown their power to control political forces that have destroyed strong men. They represent the widest variations on the global scene. The governments they head range from Communist through Democratic to Fascist. Their nations include the most developed and the least developed areas of the world. Their individual lives show even greater differences. Some have had to risk their lives for the causes they have won. Some spent many years in political prisons. Others have suffered no more than temporary eclipse in the political cycles of parliamentary governments. But their leadership in all cases proved durable enough to last while they strove to shape a new society or reshape an old one.

The leadership qualities they so obviously possess make an inviting riddle for the reader. Toughness is plainly indispensable. But they have had to be both lion and fox to keep their footing in the shifting tides of politics. Luck clearly played a role with some. It was luck to be winning independence from Britain rather than from Belgium. It was luck to be taking counter-revolution to Spain while Hitler and Mussolini were still around to lend an iron hand. Since all but two are currently in power, their careers incomplete, we cannot be sure that the luck of some may not run out. Even so, all have made an enduring mark in the histories of their countries.

It is clear that beyond toughness, luck and political dexterity, these leaders personify certain national traits. Whether it was the unflappable Mac or the impervious De Gaulle, each had personalities that could evoke the popular response that insured political success. These are representative men.

The pattern of the book would be simpler if they all represented aspirations to a larger freedom and a more democratic social order. It would be a more complex study of the cross currents of our times if some represented lost causes or the more monolithic political states. The leaders of the two vast communist empires are conspicuously omitted. But for a round dozen assorted leaders who have had a vital impact on their times, these range over a wide variety of political forms and cultural differences, and most of the continents. They include the oldest free societies, in Macmillan and De Gaulle, and the youngest in Abubakar and Bourguiba. Some sought to bring their people into the modern age, as Ataturk and Cardenas. Others had the task of restoration. But whether in West Germany or Ireland, in Israel or India, the crises of the times called for strong leadership and these men had what it took.

Through these biographical studies, Mr. Greenwald has described also the political issues and social forces that provided the background and the opportunity for these dynamic leaders.

His profiles, done originally for the educational television station, WGBH, have proved a welcome and effective form of broadcast essay and are highly suggestive of the means available to bring to television lively and informative discussion of public affairs.

Louis M. Lyons

Cambridge, Massachusetts
January, 1961

I DE GAULLE: PROPHET OF FRENCH GRANDEUR

Napoleon once remarked that "the influence of words over men is astounding." History has shown that the magic of words over and over again has caused men to subordinate their own interests and desires for some patriotic cause.

History has also shown that men sometimes bestow on their national leader an irrational, almost religious devotion, which gives him unusually great authority and influence. The German political sociologist, Max Weber, described this phenomenon as *charisma.* Those modern leaders who possess the charismatic appeal have an important advantage in persuading their countrymen to make the compromises and sacrifices which are so essential for successful government. This era of the Common Man has seen many leaders, both democratic and dictatorial, who have encouraged the "cult of the personality," but few contemporary democratic leaders are better endowed with charismatic qualities than Charles de Gaulle.

France, the oldest nation-state in Europe, is the birthplace of European nationalism. In the 17th and 18th centuries, during the reign of the Bourbon kings, France was also the cultural center of the Western world. The great French Revolution of 1789, which inaugurated the era of the common man, also sparked the birth of modern nationalism, the force which still unites and motivates a vast segment of the earth's population.

Charles de Gaulle, President of France, may well be called the prophet of French grandeur. Great is the man who can once be his country's savior, and history has twice called upon this enigmatic, inspired figure to redeem his country from chaos. Throughout his lifetime, De Gaulle has been driven by his ardent faith

1

in a strong, united France holding her rightful place among the leading nations of the world. On France's collapse in 1940, the voice of this professional soldier rose in defiance against the conquerors of his homeland, and almost alone exhorted the world to honor and respect the greatness of France. France's re-emergence and acceptance as a power after the war must be accredited to De Gaulle's stubborn insistence that the Allies give her a fully equal place among them. Again in 1958, a divided and demoralized France, threatened with military revolt, turned almost unanimously to the one man capable of reuniting her. Not since Napoleon has the French nation so fully supported a leader, nor France enjoyed such apparent unity or world prestige.

Although somewhat mystical in his near-religious devotion to France, De Gaulle has shown an astute political instinct. He is a masterful writer and historian, on a par with Churchill; he is a brilliant speaker, and possessor of a profound knowledge of mass psychology. By nature, however, he is reserved; and by personality as well as deliberate intent, he is aloof, with no close personal friends outside his family.

Charles de Gaulle was born in Lille, France in 1890 of a devout Catholic family. From an early age he showed the distinctive qualities of intellect and leadership which have marked his entire life. His father, a professor, was responsible in large part for the boy's early maturity because he treated young Charles always as an adult, discussing with him a wide range of subjects—religion, literature, politics, and especially the history of France. Due to his family's long association with the French army, De Gaulle took an early interest in military affairs, and particularly in military history. At the age of ten he was analyzing the strategy of the major battles in France. In 1909, De Gaulle entered St. Cyr, the West Point of France, and later fought with distinction in World War I.

After the war De Gaulle remained in the army as a professional soldier. In 1920 he married Yvonne Vendroux, who has been an important stabilizing influence in his life. During the war, while in a German prison, and particularly in the interwar years, De Gaulle carefully studied both German and French military tactics. He early foresaw the new mobile character of

Charles de Gaulle: "*What is henceforth of prime importance for the government is its effectiveness and its stability. We live in a time when gigantic forces are transforming the world. At the risk of becoming an obsolete and scorned people, we must develop in the scientific, economic, and social domains. Thus, it is for the people that the new constitution has been created; so that the country may be efficiently led by those whom it mandates and to whom it gives the confidence which generates legitimacy; so that it should exist above political battles, a national arbiter. . . .*"

warfare, and became an active exponent in articles and on the lecture platform of mechanizing the French army for rapid movement. French military and political leaders were cool to his proposals, but across the Rhine, German officers studied his ideas carefully, and modeled their Panzer divisions and the blitzkrieg type of warfare in great part on De Gaulle's plans.

De Gaulle also wrote extensively on French politics and history, and developed his belief that it was the historic mission of France to be the cultural and political leader of Europe.

The outbreak of World War II found De Gaulle in command of one of France's few armored divisions. In the Battle of France, De Gaulle's unit was the only one that could claim any important victory against the German blitz attack.

De Gaulle refused to acknowledge the surrender of France in May, 1940, and withdrew to Britain to carry on the French struggle against the Germans. There he quickly emerged as the acknowledged leader of French resistance. He became the head of the Free French forces, not only in England and the French possessions in Africa and the Middle East, but also in the underground of Occupied France.

Prior to 1940 De Gaulle had been virtually unknown among Frenchmen. His frequent radio messages and communications to the underground established him and his emblem, the Cross of Lorraine, as the symbols of French freedom and dignity. Even when French fortunes were at their lowest ebb, De Gaulle, with but a handful of followers, tenaciously demanded that the Allies accept Free France as an equal partner, and himself as its spokesman and leader. Churchill and Roosevelt were frequently angered by his demands for status; Churchill said, unfairly perhaps, that the Cross of Lorraine was the heaviest cross he had to bear.

In 1943 De Gaulle became head of a provisional French government, and after the Allied armies had liberated France in 1944, he returned in triumph to Paris, the leader and national hero of his country. De Gaulle then served sixteen months until early 1946 as Premier, with what amounted to dictatorial powers. Even though he was already sharply criticizing the politicians of the re-emerging parties for their pettiness and extreme partisanship, De Gaulle remained a scrupulous democrat and allowed all factions complete freedom to express their views. In this climate of political freedom, the party leaders wrote the constitution for the new Fourth Republic of France. This constitution represented an attempt to bring France and her governmental institutions up to date. Particularly in regard to welfare policies, its approach paralleled the welfare state reforms of the new Labor government in Great Britain.

This constitution, however, despite much fanfare to the contrary, was almost identical to that of the now discredited Third Republic. The basic governmental power remained in the hands of the factionalized and parochial-minded representatives in the legislature, and the authority of the executive branch, headed by the Prime Minister, was minimal. De Gaulle opposed this constitution because he believed strong executive leadership was vital for France.

The main criticism of De Gaulle as the first postwar premier of France was that he lacked an appreciation of the relationship between economics and politics. His government did not carry out monetary reforms to weed out wartime profiteers, nor did it institute tax laws which would have placed the burden of government fairly on all classes. The widespread evasion of tax payment, an old French custom carried over from the Third Republic, continued unchecked. Despite the pleas of his very capable Minister for Economic Affairs, Mendes-France, De Gaulle almost ignored this situation. France seemed to be reverting to the old attitudes and cynicism which had so weakened the Third Republic.

While he was premier, De Gaulle continued to press the Allies to give his nation an equal voice among them in the post-war settlements. Somewhat reluctantly, they gave France a zone of occupation in Germany, and admitted her to the Occupation Government. In the newly-formed United Nations, France was given a seat as a permanent member of the Security Council with the United States, Great Britain, the Soviet Union, and Nationalist China.

When the Constitution of the Fourth Republic went into effect in January, 1946, De Gaulle resigned as premier and went into retirement. He predicted, however, that this new constitution could not last.

In April, 1947, De Gaulle marked his return to politics by announcing that he was determined to give France a new constitution which would rid her once and for all of the damaging consequences of party maneuvering and bickering. He now proclaimed the formation of the "Rally of the French People" (*Rassemblement du Peuple Francais*), a movement which, in De Gaulle's words, would "promote the union of our people and the reform of our state over and above national division."

A great number of Frenchmen responded to his appeal, and with Jacques Soustelle as its organizing head, this movement became almost immediately a major force in French politics. Within six months, it was the largest party in the country.

The Rally of the French People sought to strengthen national unity and to provide for an effective executive. Its appeal was, therefore, a nationalist one. In France, attitudes such as those of the RPF have traditionally been the position of the anti-democratic rightist parties. Although the leaders of the RPF, obviously including De Gaulle, had not cooperated with the Nazis in World War II, many former collaborators of the Right aligned themselves with this movement. The RPF also frequently showed impatience with, and contempt of, democratic procedures associated with parliamentary government.

De Gaulle soon discovered, however, that his party was being weakened by parliamentary intrigue and factionalism in its own ranks. In 1951 he again, in effect, retired from politics, and the RPF soon dissolved.

For the next seven years, De Gaulle remained in seclusion in his country home, seldom speaking out on public issues. He closely followed French and world affairs, however, and maintained contact with key leaders of the defunct RPF. He remained supremely confident that the Fourth Republic would not be able to carry on and that he would again be called upon to lead France.

True to his expectations the French Fourth Republic collapsed in 1958, because it failed to stabilize the country internally, and was unable to resolve France's place in a world dominated by two super-powers. The declining prestige of the successive ministries of the Fourth Republic caused increased partisanship to arise among the many divisions in French society: farmers, laborers, small shopkeepers, clerics, and anti-clerics. Particularly after 1954, a series of overseas events occurred which weakened the confidence of large segments of the French population in their government. The French Army, supported by a minority of extreme nationalists, especially among the French settlers in Algeria, was the direct cause of the downfall of the Fourth Republic. The army's officer corps had grown increasingly resentful toward the politicians in Paris for not giving them adequate support in holding France's overseas possessions. The decision to withdraw from Indo-China provoked many army officers, particularly when a sizable portion of that area was taken over by the Communist rebels. French disenchantment grew with the realization by more and more people that France had become a second-rate power. The Algerian revolt, starting in 1954, was the final blow. The intelligent desire of this political leadership in Paris to conciliate, and to come to terms with the Algerian nationalist rebels, horrified the French officers there who were encouraged by French Algerian settlers and ultra-nationalists in France to defy their civilian superiors. In the spring of 1958, the army came out in open defiance of the Paris government, and France seemed in danger of a military coup.

A great majority of the parliamentary leaders recognized that De Gaulle alone had the prestige to command the obedience of the army, and with few dissenters, they called upon him to become Premier. Assuming office on June 1, 1958, De Gaulle quickly proceeded to take command of the situation and to prepare a new constitution for a Fifth Republic.

A party was formed, calling itself the Union for the New Republic, guided by former leaders of the Rally of the French People. Its all-out support of De Gaulle has given the UNR its only coherence or unity. This party has had a broader base of diverse interests and has not had the antidemocratic bias of the RPF. It is the bandwagon on which politicians have jumped in order to capitalize on De Gaulle's popularity.

In September, De Gaulle submitted his newly drafted constitution to a general referendum of all French voters. This constitution provided for a greatly strengthened executive and a correspondingly weaker legislature. Tailored for himself, the constitution vested real executive authority in the president, rather than in the premier.

On September 28, 1958, the French voted on De Gaulle's constitution and over 82 per cent of them approved it. The following December De Gaulle's prestige was upheld when he was overwhelmingly elected first president of the Fifth French Republic.

Since his second rise to power, De Gaulle has striven to heal the economic and political wounds that afflict French society. He has given France strong leadership, but he has respected democratic rights. He has consciously tried to be less aloof in his dealings with subordinates, and to convey a more democratic public image of himself. In reality many of De Gaulle's political goals have been the same as those of the Fourth Republic's leaders, but his charismatic appeal and his greater executive authority have given him more success in achieving them.

Under De Gaulle the economic boom which started in France in 1954, and which was the handiwork of Fourth Republic leaders, has continued and even expanded. De Gaulle has shown that he profited from the mistakes of his premiership from 1944-46. Now he shows an awareness of the importance of economics, and has devoted much of his energy to placing France on a sound economic basis. He inaugurated a farsighted and long-overdue program of equalizing the tax burden. With his greater prestige, De Gaulle has been able to weaken the political influence of the reactionary farm and small business blocs, and has accelerated the automization of French industry and agriculture. For the first time since the war, French currency has been stabilized and the trend toward inflation diminished. France today has one of the highest standards of living in Western Europe.

One sign of France's industrial advance and of her determination to be a great power is her atomic energy program. Since the earliest days of the Fourth Republic, French leaders have sought to bring France into the "Atomic Club" of the United States, Britain, and the Soviet Union; in February, 1960, the French, ignoring all hostile world opinion on the subject, exploded their first atomic bomb. France thereby became the world's fourth atomic power. Both in and out of power, De Gaulle strongly supported this program. He has clearly wanted the bomb for use as political leverage in compelling the Soviet Union and the Western Allies alike to respect French power.

With his constitution, De Gaulle inaugurated a new relationship with France's overseas possessions. A French Community was established, somewhat on the pattern of the British Commonwealth. Overseas possessions, except Algeria, were given the opportunity to govern themselves either in union with France through the Community or, if their people so voted, in complete independence. Only one area, Guinea, chose to break completely with France, the remainder of France's vast holdings electing to retain their ties within the framework of the French Community. France is directing much of her foreign economic and technical assistance to these republics, probably for reasons of prestige as much as for any economic motive France may have.

The greatest challenge to De Gaulle's leadership continues to be the chronic problem of Algeria. The nationalist revolt there has been gong on since 1954, and has cost France billions of dollars. Also, by tying up most of the army, it has weakened France's military position in NATO. The French settlers in Algeria have remained the most reactionary element in French politics, and have more and more denounced De Gaulle as a traitor to their interests —just as they had previously denounced the politicians of the Fourth Republic. De Gaulle's policy has been to seek common ground with the well-organized leaders of the revolt. He has also compelled the army, a stronghold of ultra-nationalist sentiment, to submit to civilian control. Some of his own followers, notably Jacques Soustelle, have broken with De Gaulle because of the latter's alleged appeasement of the rebels, and particularly because he has been willing to meet and negotiate openly with such key rebel leaders as Ferhat Abbas.

To most outsiders, it seems doubtful that any solution to the Algerian problem can be found short of complete French military withdrawal. De Gaulle has not accepted this solution, but has searched for compromise solutions which so far have been unacceptable to either side, although both sides respect his sincerity. During his December, 1960, visit to Algeria he was cheered even by the rebels for his courage in trying to gain support for his referendum. The French colons were cool to any prospect of relinquishing their position in Algeria, however, and it is doubtful whether De Gaulle will be able to obtain genuine cooperation from them in his plan for Algerian self-determination. Despite this, there has been growing popular support for De Gaulle's approach to the problem. No doubt his eloquence, and his ability to rally widely divergent elements of French opinion, have greatly contributed to this support. In his television appeal to the people of France and Algeria on December 20, 1960, De Gaulle expressed his determination to find a peaceful and democratic solution to the Algerian crisis:

> The French people are . . . called upon to say . . . through the referendum, whether they approve—as I ask them to—that as soon as peace reign, the Algerian populations choose their own destiny. That means: either to break with the French Republic, to be a part of it, or to be associated with it, [through the French Community]. . . . The Algeria of tomorrow, then, will be Algerian. The Algerians will conduct their own affairs, and it will be up to them alone to found a state with its own government, its own constitutions, and its own laws.

De Gaulle's political future may well be decided by his handling of the Algerian question. Will even his political and military genius prove equal to this situation? Or will Algeria prove to be the stumbling block to the fulfillment of De Gaulle's grandiose dream of restoring France to her pre-eminent position in world affairs—to the *gloire* that was hers in the helday of her great kings?

II MACMILLAN: TRAVELING DIPLOMAT
IN THE SERVICE OF PEACE

Britain's Prime Minister Harold Macmillan will probably go down in history as one of the 20th century's most capable and influential statesmen. At home, he has commanded more popular support than any other prime minister since World War II; while abroad he has gained respect from both East and West as a tireless "traveling diplomat" in the service of peace.

Macmillan's scholarly, sophisticated manner stamps him as an "egghead" by American standards. Moreover, adhering to the finest tradition of English eloquence, Macmillan is known as one of Britain's most polished speakers. In other respects also, he typifies the urbanity, wit, and refinement of taste that are the distinctive marks of the English gentleman. His own countrymen call him "unflappable"—meaning that he is calm and unmoved by either success or catastrophe.

Macmillan is a director of the great Macmillan publishing house founded by his grandfather. By marriage he is connected with one of England's most aristocratic families. Yet he has been for many years the advocate of democratic social reforms, and for a long time was critical of the Conservative Party's opposition to welfare legislation. Macmillan sometimes gives the appearance of being sedate and cold when he speaks in public; but in informal discussion he projects great warmth and human feeling. Because he is a fastidious dresser, a lover of lively and witty conversation, and is, unashamedly, a *bon vivant,* he was regarded early in his career by many as simply a well-to-do playboy and political dilettante, reminiscent of a bygone aristocratic era. But his integrity, ability, and seriousness very quickly dispelled this first impression—especially so when he became Prime Minister. The Labor opposition has tacitly

11

Harold Macmillan: "... *Both sides should have an understanding of the other side's point of view. We didn't agree about many important issues, but I think we did agree about this, which is to me the supreme issue of all: that these grave problems ... ought to be settled by negotiation and not by force. ...*"

acknowledged Macmillan's great prestige by generally refraining from direct criticism of him personally, preferring to concentrate its attacks on the Conservative Party as a whole. Thus Macmillan has succeeded in projecting himself as a father figure in Britain, just as Eisenhower has done in the United States.

Perhaps Macmillan's major claim to fame is that he is the best example and now the leading spokesman of the so-called "New Conservatism"—the term used to describe the basic changes in political philosophy and policy that now characterize the Conservative Party. That party today is fully committed to a welfare state program, including such government services as unemployment and health insurance, and old age and retirement benefits. Nevertheless, it remains somewhat a class party representing the higher income groups, and business and commercial interests. Postwar political realities and the social consciousness of many Conservative leaders have so radically transformed this historic party that today it makes its appeal to all segments of the British population. Indeed, now that the British Labor Party is dropping its commitment to total nationalization of industry, there does not seem to be any serious ideological difference between the two parties. They are today closer in outlook on the key issues than at any time since Labor emerged as the main opposition party.

In Britain, the Conservative Party—formerly called the Tory Party—has been the traditional defender of Church, Crown, and Constitution. For historical reasons it is informally aligned with the Church of England, and members of this Church tend to be more sympathetic toward the Conservative cause. For the same historic reasons, Nonconformists have tended to align themselves with the party opposing the Conservatives. In the 19th and early 20th centuries the Liberal Party was the great foe of the Conservatives. The Liberals, representing the rising industrial class, were critical of some of the old Conservative attitudes. The Conservatives drew much of their strength from the powerful old aristocratic families. However, the Liberal Party—unlike the emerging Labor Party—was not committed to any sweeping program of reform or abstract doctrine. While seeking a more substantial voice in government affairs for the new commercial interests, the Liberals did not wish to alter radically the Conservative order of things.

The end of World War I saw the Labor Party displace the Liberals as the major opposition party. The Labor Party, although a moderate and evolutionary socialist party, was nonetheless also a class party, striving to represent the working people and the underprivileged classes in general. In 1945, Labor won its first decisive victory, and under Clement Attlee a Labor government ruled Britain for five years. Under this government large-scale welfare programs were inaugurated and expanded, and many of the major industries in Britain were nationalized. In great part because of their decisive defeat in 1945, but also because of changes in thinking caused by the dislocations and sacrifices of the war effort, the leaders of the Conservative Party formulated a basically new program and outlook. Most of the innovations of the Labor government were accepted, and some even enlarged upon. Macmillan was one of a number of younger Conservative leaders who worked for this "New Conservatism."

Today the main difference between the Conservatives and Labor is that the Conservatives have a more flexible and pragmatic political outlook, yet, like the Republican Party in the United States, the Conservatives in Britain speak more favorably of free enterprise and rugged individualism than do their opponents.

The Conservative Party, with its "new look," has won three successive elections (1951, 1955, and 1959), and in each has increased its strength over Labor. Macmillan was an advocate of this new look for the Conservative Party long before it had become fashionable with the party's leadership. By the early 1930's he was one of a small number of militant and outspoken Conservatives who wished to bring the party to accept greater responsibility for the welfare of the individual British citizen.

Harold Macmillan was born in 1894 of an American mother and a Scottish father. He received a classical education at Eton and Oxford and served with distinction in World War I. In 1920, he married Lady Dorothy Cavendish. They have three daughters and one son who is a member of Parliament. Macmillan has been in politics almost all his adult life, first entering Parliament in 1924. The district he represented, Stockton-on-Tees, was in a region of Britain hard hit by unemployment and general economic distress. It was here that he developed many of his ideas on social reform and greater economic equality. The great depression of 1929 caused Macmillan to prod his party to develop energetic and imaginative methods of combating unemployment and other social ills. He became a sharp critic of the two important inter-war leaders of the conservatives, Stanley Baldwin and Neville Chamberlain.

While still a young man Macmillan had come under the influence of the great liberal economist, John Maynard Keynes, and had begun to share many of Keynes' ideas on the government's responsibility to maintain and encourage economic prosperity.

As early as 1934, Macmillan called upon his party to recognize the dynamic task the present generation must accomplish; this, he said, included the conquest of poverty, the abolition of insecurity, the stabilization of prosperity, and the discovery of new social devices for the regulation of plenty. In 1938, he published a book, *The Middle Way*, which summarized his welfare state ideas.

Macmillan actively opposed the foreign policy of the Conservative Party leadership during the 1930's. Like Churchill, he very early became alarmed at the menace of Nazi Germany and fought the appeasement policies of Neville Chamberlain. So strong was his opposition that he in effect withdrew from the Conservative Party and on one occasion aligned himself with the left wing of the Labor Party in opposing the policy of Chamberlain.

When Churchill succeeded Chamberlain in 1940, Macmillan returned to the Conservative Party and was given a ministerial position by Churchill. In 1942, he was assigned to North Africa as a key political representative. There he worked closely with General Eisenhower, and the two developed a warm friendship. By the end of the war he had held a number of important positions in Italy, Greece, and France, and was established as an important Conservative Party leader.

A key turning-point in his career occurred in 1951 when Macmillan was appointed Minister of Housing in Churchill's cabinet. The year before, the annual Conservative Party Conference had rather rashly pledged itself to build 300,000 new homes annually, a figure far in excess of what the previous Labor government had shown itself able to do. Macmillan took this commitment seriously and proceeded to have built 300,000 houses per year, somewhat to the embarrassment of many economy-minded people in Britain. His success in handling this situation led to his advancement to the posts of minister of defense, foreign secretary, chancellor of the exchequer—Britain's equivalent of our Secretary of the Treasury—and finally in January, 1957, at the height of the Suez crisis, he was chosen to replace Anthony Eden as prime minister.

The Conservative Party had suffered considerable loss of prestige as a result of the Suez crisis; Macmillan managed, not only to recover the party's prestige, but to increase its political power to perhaps a higher point than at any time in the post-war period. A prime minister in Britain must be the effective leader of his party in order to maintain himself in power. He usually is faced with a number of factions and much grumbling within his party's ranks. Most recent Conservative prime ministers—Stanley Baldwin in the 1920's, Chamberlain in the 1930's, and Eden in the 1950's—have faced considerable discontent and even open rebellion within their party. Macmillan, however, very quickly earned himself the enthusiastic support of almost all of his party's members in the House of Commons.

One of the main reasons for Macmillan's success as prime minister is that he is a skilled administrator and knows how to delegate authority to his subordinates. He makes key decisions himself and then allows his subordinates free rein and full opportunity to perform their duties. This policy has regularly earned him the staunch loyalty of the men under him.

Television has been an important source of Macmillan's political strength. He has shown a remarkable ability to project his personality and win the confidence, and presumably the political support, of great numbers of Englishmen. Curiously, it was the American television commentators, Charles Collingwood and Edward R. Murrow, who guided Macmillan in presenting himself in an informal way to the television audience. His frequent TV appearances, where he generally speaks without a formally prepared script, are reminiscent of the late Franklin Roosevelt's fireside chats. On August 31, 1959, on the eve of his first general election as prime minister, Macmillan made a widely-heralded television appearance with President Eisenhower. This casual discussion between the two sincere and fatherly leaders on the great issues of the day was telecast all over Britain and in much of Western Europe. It made a strongly favorable impression for Macmillan, undoubtedly contributing to his great election victory the following October.

Macmillan has also sought to develop the so-called "common touch." He has regularly traveled through Britain, visiting factories, farms, and private institutions of various sorts and chatting with people in all walks of life. Macmillan relishes the give and take of British politics and has shown himself a master in answering hecklers. In campaigning, he always manages to preserve his wit and good humor.

One of Macmillan's main concerns as prime minister has been to strengthen the Western Alliance of Nations, especially the bond between the United States and Great Britain. Anglo-American friendship, the heart of the Western Alliance, was badly strained during the Suez crisis. The United States had criticized and opposed British intervention in Egypt. In his efforts to restore good relations, Macmillan conferred with President Eisenhower and John Foster Dulles in Bermuda in March, 1957. In October of the same year, with his Foreign Secretary, Selwyn Lloyd, Macmillan visited Eisenhower and Dulles in Washington and there they issued a "Declaration of Common Purpose" pledging mutual support and cooperation in resolving world problems. Thereafter Macmillan held frequent personal conferences with President Eisenhower. Partly because of Macmillan's efforts, United States-British relations are again closer than at any time since World War II.

In the same spirit, Macmillan has striven to maintain closer official and personal ties with the other leaders of the Western Alliance, especially De Gaulle of France and Adenauer of Germany. In the Western Summit Meeting of December, 1959, the purpose of which was to formulate the West's united approach for the May, 1960, Summit Meeting with Khruschchev, Macmillan was already the most forceful and articulate figure.

One thing that has separated Great Britain from France and Germany has been the question of the Common Market. Italy, Belgium, the Netherlands, and Luxembourg, led by France and Germany, are setting up what amounts to an economic United States of Europe. Britain has been unwilling to join this Common Market, in great part because of her ties and commitments to the members of her Commonwealth. Macmillan, however, because of his interest in Western unity, and because he, like De Gaulle and Adenauer, is a "European" and sympathetic to the idea of an effective European union, has considered cooperating with, and even joining, the Common Market. However, many of the Conservative leaders, are opposed to subordinating Britain's interests within the Common Market.

On becoming Prime Minister, Macmillan inaugurated a policy of relaxation of economic controls in Great Britain even though as Chancellor of the Exchequer several years before, he had earned the nickname "Mac the Knife" because of his vigorous control policies. By 1957, he advocated dropping much of the currency control, buying and selling regulations, and the credit restrictions limiting the British economy. Some members of his own party opposed this and his chancellor of the exchequer resigned because of it; but this policy was generally received with great favor by the majority of the population. Britain, so far at least, has prospered under it.

Macmillan's overriding concern as prime minister has been to end the cold war between East and West. He has by no means favored appeasement, yet, more than any other important Western leader, he has worked to find common ground for agreement with the Soviet Union. He is greatly apprehensive about the dangers of nuclear warfare for the entire world and particularly for Britain. He recognizes that Britain, a small, crowded island, would be almost totally destroyed in the event of nuclear warfare.

In February and March of 1959, Macmillan made a widely heralded visit to the Soviet Union. He held conferences with Khrushchev and other Soviet leaders and visited many different parts of Russia. He was given an opportunity to speak over Moscow's TV station and very ably presented the Western position to the Russian people. He hailed the economic progress of the Soviet Union but emphasized that the Western nations were still ahead in per capita production, especially in consumer goods. "We as a nation," he said, "live by trade; there you have a key to understanding our approach to affairs. A nation living by trade needs peace." He also defended the British political system and its freedoms and pointed out that it was more than satisfactory for British needs. Without directly criticizing the Soviet dictatorship, he stressed that, in the British view, free and secret elections, freedom of discussion, and toleration in public affairs were absolute necessities for real democratic government.

He strongly urged the improvement of British-Soviet relations and advocated increased tourism between the Soviet Union and the West as a means of bettering mutual understanding.

From the summer of 1958 on, Macmillan had been working hard to arrange for a summit talk between East and West. His persuasion was partly responsible for Eisenhower's decision to attend the summit meeting scheduled for May, 1960.

In Paris, Macmillan bent every effort to prevent the break-up of the summit conference over the American U2 spy-plane incident. Even after the failure of the Summit and the Soviet Union's subsequent withdrawal from the disarmament conference in Geneva, Macmillan has sought ways of resuming negotiations. Although he has sharply criticized Khrushchev for his unreasonableness, he has left the door open for future discussion.

Macmillan has recognized the importance of the Afro-Asian peoples in the cold-war struggle with the Soviet Union. As a leader of the Commonwealth, he has visited India, Southeast Asia, and toured Africa in early 1960. He has recognized the African people's desire for an end to colonial rule and has been liberal and farsighted in granting independence to Britain's African possessions. While in South Africa he showed political courage by sharply criticizing the discriminatory policies of the white South African government. He declared the urgency of recognizing and dealing intelligently with the "winds of change" that are sweeping through Africa if that continent is to be won to the side of the free world.

Thus, by bringing to bear all the power and prestige of his great office upon the most critical areas of world tension, and by exercising his talents of persuasion, tact, and political compromise, Macmillan has managed to preserve Britain's position as a leading member of the free world coalition.

Konrad Adenauer: ". . . I am beset by the anxiety that the free peoples of this world would forfeit their freedom if they were to accept as an unalterable fact the present state of affairs prevailing in the world and were to slide into a period of weakness and disunity in the face of the uniform, ruthless, and purely power greedy policy of the East. . . ."

III ADENAUER: ARCHITECT OF
FRANCO-GERMAN UNITY

The Bible tells us that the days of our years are three score and ten. But in 1949 Konrad Adenauer, at the age of 73, became chancellor of West Germany, and for more than a decade he has dominated German politics. West Germany's amazing economic recovery, her policy of friendship and alliance with the West, have been in large part the handiwork of this remarkable statesman. Adenauer, a devout Catholic, has been driven by his deeply-rooted religious principles to rebuild Germany on a more humane and ethical foundation.

If West Germany evolves, in spirit as well as in form, into a democracy, much of the credit will belong to Adenauer. Although he has an iron-willed, somewhat authoritarian personality, he is nevertheless a convinced believer in democracy. He has given Germany strong and efficient leadership within a democratic framework.

On the negative side, Adenauer may be critized for frustrating the development of a truly effective democratic legislature in Germany through his use of high-handed political tactics. Yet his efforts to bind Germany forever with the rest of Western Europe may prove ultimately to be the route by which the German people will achieve both democracy and stability—two conditions which the Germans have never enjoyed simultaneously.

Adenauer is an ardent European; he has said that he is a European first and a German second. It would be too much to hope that his successors remain as deeply committed to the cause of the western democracies and of European unity as he has been.

Adenauer is a reserved, self-contained man. He dislikes sentimentality, and is at times impatient and severe with his subordinates. Throughout his life he has pursued his goals with fanatical drive and determination. Adenauer is also a perfectionist. "Nothing is well done which is half done," he has said. Nevertheless, he has also shown remarkable flexibility and adaptability. He is receptive to new ideas and new faces. He has that unusual capacity for listening patiently, sympathetically, to the views of others. *Der Alte*—"the old man" —as he is affectionately called, is regarded by most Germans with a respect they have accorded only a handful of German statesmen during their long history of political leaders, good and bad.

Although austere and forceful in public, Adenauer's private life exemplifies the *Gemuetlichkeit*—that enjoyment of good food, warmth, and companionship—that is best in the German character. He is also greatly interested in art and literature. Like Macmillan, he has a profound knowledge of European and world history. His understanding of the German past guides him in his efforts to influence the future.

Adenauer's power comes from his leadership of Germany's largest party, the Christian Democratic Union. He was one of the organizers of this party, which has sought to unite politically both Catholics and Protestants. Adenauer and others who founded the Christian Democratic Union had been members of the pre-war German Center Party. The Center Party had been established in Germany in the latter part of the 19th century by Roman Catholics to protect their interests against the Protestant government of Imperial Germany. Its membership was almost entirely Catholic, and church officials had considerable direct influence on the policies of the Center Party. The present Christian Democratic Union has striven to unite Protestants and Catholics and has kept itself largely free of direct church influence.

The CDU is also more fully committed to democracy than was the Center Party. Parties similar in makeup to the CDU have also played leading roles in the governments of Italy and France in the post-war period. The Catholic leaders of the Italian and French Christian Democratic parties have shared many of Adenauer's convictions regarding European cooperation and economic union. One of the most hopeful events of recent European history—the French-German reconciliation—has been greatly facilitated by the common political outlook of the Christian Democratic leaders of these two countries.

Adenauer's life for a long time revolved around the city of Cologne. Situated in the Rhine valley near the borders of France, this predominantly Catholic city has long been a center of German liberalism. Adenauer was born here in 1876 of a lower-middle class family. Even as a very young man, he showed the driving energy and determination which have characterized his political life. He worked his way through high school and university, studying administration and law. After briefly serving as a prosecuting attorney and privately practicing law, Adenauer, already an active member of the Center Party, entered the Cologne city government in 1906. In 1904, he had married Emma Weyer, a member of a socially prominent and influential Cologne family. In 1917, he became mayor of Cologne and served in this position until he was deposed by Hitler in 1933.

As the mayor of Cologne, Adenauer developed the general methods and policies which now characterize his Chancellorship. Although he gave Cologne an efficient and honest administration, he was often then, as he is now, impatient with those who opposed him. In 1927, although Adenauer was decisively outvoted by the Cologne Municipal Council on the minor issue of a suspension bridge, he skillfully managed to frustrate the Council and reverse the decision.

The horrors of World War I and the post-war revolutions in Germany very early convinced Adenauer that the new Germany must be guided by the Christian spirit and must maintain friendship and peace with her neighbors. Particularly with France, Germany's traditional enemy, Adenauer urged good relations. In the early 1920's he was considered by many German nationalists as a Separatist—one who favored the union of the highly industrialized Rhineland with France, or at least the neutralization of this area. Although he was not actually a Separatist, his conciliatory attitude toward France and French fears of Germany reflected his determination in pursuing a Franco-German understanding.

While still in Cologne, he continually urged German Catholics and Protestants to submerge their historic religious animosities which divided Germany politically and socially. Also at this time, as a consequence of the left-wing socialist uprisings which occurred in Cologne and other German cities in 1918-19, Adenauer developed his present deeply-rooted aversion to doctrinaire socialism.

By 1926 he had become an important national political figure and was established as a key leader of the Center Party. In that year President Hindenburg offered him the chancellorship of Germany, but because of bitter party differences Adenauer was not able to obtain the necessary parliamentary majority to take office.

Adenauer the mayor strongly opposed the rising Nazi Party, in part because of its atheism, and also because of its emphasis on extreme militarism and nationalism. Soon after being appointed Chancellor in 1933, Hitler made a state visit to Cologne. Adenauer, contemptuous of the Nazis, stubbornly refused to allow his city to be decorated with Nazi banners. Hitler immediately had him deposed.

Adenauer did not support the Nazi regime, but since he believed that resistance to it was futile from 1933 on, he did not actively oppose it.

The American forces who captured Cologne near the end of the war soon reinstated Adenauer as mayor. Cologne, however, was assigned to the British zone of Germany, and its British commander fired Adenauer and for a short time restricted his political freedom. By this action the British unwittingly helped Adenauer to achieve his present position of power; for only after they relieved him of his responsibility of the office of mayor did Adenauer have the free time to campaign for the chancellorship. Moreover the incident brought him into the limelight, and convinced the Germans that he was not a mere stooge of the Allied powers.

Adenauer proceeded to organize the new Christian Democratic Union, drawing much support from members of the pre-war Center Party. In Cologne he quickly became the acknowledged leader of a strong CDU group. He also traveled throughout West Germany, organizing and guiding the formation of this new party.

By 1948 Adenauer was established as the CDU's number-one man. In the three-year period since the war Adenauer had revitalized himself. Constantly on the go, he traveled 100,000 miles annually, attending meetings and conferences. Moving at a pace that would have exhausted a much younger man, he seemed to increase in strength and vigor.

Under Adenauer's leadership the CDU emerged a well-organized, disciplined political party, the largest in Germany. When the new West German Federal Republic was inaugurated in September, 1949, Adenauer became its first chancellor.

Since then he has dominated German politics. His strong position of control over the policies and finances of the CDU has assured him control of the German parliament. Moreover, the West German constitution, written under his guidance, gives great executive authority to the chancellor to avoid the governmental instability which characterized the 1920's. The German public, because of its great respect for Adenauer and because of Germany's long tradition of strong executive leadership, tends to accept Adenauer's policies without question. Adenauer has the successful politician's instinct for publicity, and he has done much to encourage popular and parliamentary support for himself and his policies with a highly organized public relations program.

Many of his opponents, and supporters as well, have criticized Adenauer's authoritarian methods in his relations with Parliament and his ministers. Many observers fear that German democracy may collapse after Adenauer leaves the scene. A British newspaperman, Brian Connell, has observed that the present German prosperity, which is the basis for Adenauer's successful regime, has been founded on the industry, discipline, and respect for authority of the German people. "If the Germans in defeat," he says, "have not forgotten the virtues of hard work, they have learned little new." Although Adenauer's methods may often be criticized for having retarded the growth of German democracy, he has given Germany a long period of the prosperity and stability which are absolute prerequisites to the development of a truly democratic German state.

Germany today is essentially a two-party state, like the United States and Great Britain. The Social Democratic Party is the primary opposition party to the CDU. The CDU is still troubled by sharp factional differences within its ranks, a problem which also bedeviled the old Center Party. Although discipline is now rigid in the CDU because of Adenauer, without his leadership there is a strong possibility that the party will break up or, even worse, be taken over by undemocratic elements.

The opposition Social Democrats have very recently dropped their doctrinaire Marxist outlook and adopted a more pragmatic approach to domestic politics. They have given up their demands for widespread nationalization of industry. In their approach to domestic and foreign affairs, including even such a controversial issue as the remilitarization of Germany, they are basically in accord with Adenauer and the Christian Democrats.

The outstanding post-war figure among the Social Democrats was Kurt Schumacher, who died in 1952. A man of great intelligence and political ability, he was, like Adenauer, a strong personality and a master of parliamentary maneuvering. He was one of the few leaders who could successfully compete with Adenauer in political debate. The current leading figure in the SDP is Willy Brandt, the young and very forceful mayor of West Berlin. Adenauer, ever the astute politician, is increasingly aware of Brandt's growing popularity and influence with the German voters.

In 1959, at the age of 83, Adenauer announced that he would give up the chancellorship and accept the more honorary position of president. After some reflection, however, he shocked younger political hopefuls by reversing himself, declaring that he was still needed by his party and his country as chancellor.

All of Adenauer's political energies have been directed to the establishment of a united Western Europe with a sovereign Germany as a free and equal member. Even in the early days of Allied occupation, Adenauer simultaneously struggled with the Allies for recognition of German equality, and also with German nationalists who opposed his policy of close cooperation with Western Europe.

In 1955, Adenauer's twin objectives were achieved when the Western Powers recognized Germany as a sovereign, independent nation and at the same time admitted West Germany to NATO.

Since its establishment, the Federal Republic of West Germany has been a leading member of all the important groups and organizations working to unite Europe into a tightly-knit political, economic, and military union. With France in 1952, Germany joined the European Coal and Steel Community, which sought to pool and co-ordinate Western European coal and steel production.   In 1954, Germany agreed to join the European Defense Community, which would have pooled the armies of Western Europe into one co-ordinated unit.   The French, however, decided against this, and the plan came to nothing.   Germany's admission to NATO in the following year, however, accomplished many of the objectives of the EDC.

An important step in cementing French-German relations was achieved by the Saar settlement in 1957.   The Saar, a small but important coal-mining region situated on the borders of the two countries, had been a source of controversy for 50 years.   In the settlement France was given valuable mining and transport concessions in exchange for the admission of the Saar as a member state of the German Federal Republic.

The most significant effort for uniting Europe in the post-war years has been the Common Market which came into effect on January 1, 1959.   This economic "United States of Europe" aims at achieving an open trade area without economic frontiers in Western Europe.   Adenauer has fought for all of these means to European unity, especially the Common Market, even though his advisors, particularly the capable Minister of Economic Affairs, Ludwig Erhard, have often opposed these plans as weakening Germany economically or politically.   It is doubtful that West Germany would have entered the Common Market without Adenauer's leadership.

The strong moral basis of Adenauer's character is illustrated in the reparations agreement with Israel which was passed under his guidance in 1952.   West Germany agreed to pay Israel 822 million dollars to compensate her for the settlement of several hundred thousand refugees from Nazi persecution.   Adenauer described this agreement as a moral obligation for all Germans because of the immeasurable suffering wrought upon the Jews in Germany and in the occupied countries under Nazism.   He has also caused West Germany to assume considerable financial and moral responsibility for many other victims of the Nazi regime.

Adenauer is an uncompromising opponent of Communism.   His attitude is in great part based on the division of Germany by the victorious World War II Allies.   A sizable part of pre-war

Germany, areas East of the Oder-Neisse Rivers, was in effect given to Poland. Most of the remainder of Germany was divided into two main areas, the Soviet Zone and the Western Allied Zone. The Soviet Zone has been transformed into the *German Democratic Republic,* theoretically independent, but actually a Soviet satellite. (The Western Zone has become Adenauer's the *Federal Republic of Germany.*)

The desire to unite East and West Germany has permeated German political thinking, and has been the main source of controversy between the Soviet Union and the West in Europe. Berlin, also divided into East and West sectors, but situated in the heart of the East German Soviet satellite, has further aggravated this problem. Moreover, about 13 million Germans have fled to West Germany from the East since 1945. Of these, 10 million are expellees, about 2 million having been driven from their homes in the Sudetan region of Czechoslovakia, and the remainder having been forced to flee the Polish-occupied areas of Eastern Germany. Another 3 million Germans, residents of the East German Soviet satellite, have sought refuge in West Germany. These expellees and refugees have formed a hard core of anti-Soviet sentiment in West Germany; and were it not for the economic boom which has created conditions of full employment and relative prosperity, these Germans from the East would be an even more explosive element in West German politics.

Adenauer opposed the first summit meeting held in Geneva in 1955 between Western and Soviet leaders and looked with suspicion on the thaw in East-West relations, believing that the Soviet leaders were simply adopting new tactics, but had not changed their basic objectives. Adenauer was particularly skeptical of the second summit conference which was scheduled for May 1960. He feared that Western leaders like Macmillan might be taken in by Khrushchev's seeming reasonableness and make major concessions on Germany, especially Berlin.

Adenauer has set Germany on the road to democracy. Whether or not Germany continues along this path will not detract from the greatness of his contribution.

IV FRANCO OF SPAIN: FASCIST GENERALISSIMO

The French Revolution introduced to Western Europe, among other things, the era of the bourgeousie; that is, the period of dominance of the new middle class. This era has seen the rapid urbanization and industrialization of the major Western European nations.

Liberalism was the main economic and political philosophy of the emerging middle class. The liberal political philosophy, especially in Europe, has placed prime emphasis on individualism; it has opposed most forms of governmental restraints, either of an economic or political nature. The doctrine of *laissez-faire*—hands off the businessman—is the heart and soul of the liberal economic credo. The concepts of social equality, freedom of expression, and freedom of religion were other important ingredients of the liberal philosophy, in both European and American thought. In Europe, however, though not in the United States, liberal ideas were opposed by deeply entrenched traditionalist forces, such as the established church, a landed nobility, and other vestiges of a feudal social structure which kept the peasantry in subjection. It was inevitable, therefore, that liberalism in Europe would develop along much more doctrinaire lines than it would in the United States. An emphasis on rugged individualism made liberalism in actual practice a conservative economic force, but in the political sphere, because of European liberalism's ardent advocacy of individual rights and freedom, it was, for a time, a radical element. Especially in regard to organized religion, its individualistic approach has made European liberalism strongly anti-clerical.

On the eve of World War I, in those Western European countries such as Great Britain, France, and the Scandinavian nations,

29

Francisco Franco: "We are the actors in a new era in which we can have no truck with the mentality of the past. . . . It is necessary for Spaniards to abandon old liberal prejudices. . . . The liberal world is going down, a victim of its own errors."

where there was a large and prosperous middle class, liberalism as an economic and political doctrine reigned supreme. In Central and Southern Europe, including Spain, where the middle class was smaller and weaker, liberal ideas, although influential, were strongly opposed by powerful elements of the clergy, the nobility and the landowning classes.

The new socialist movements, reflecting the political frustration of the small but growing industrial working class, rejected both the traditional order of society, represented by the church and the nobility, and the liberal order, represented by the middle class. The ideas of Karl Marx on class struggle and on the inevitability of a proletarian revolution struck their deepest roots, not in those countries that were the most advanced industrially, as Marx had anticipated, but rather in the backward, feudalistic states of Eastern and Southern Europe.

World War I, the first total war of modern times, saw a new political form develop which challenged liberalism. This was totalitarianism, which calls for the total mobilization of the human and economic resources of a nation for the purpose of achieving a specific set of national goals. Totalitarianism has taken two opposing forms, both of which, however, are strongly anti-liberal. The first of these is communism, based on Marx's theory of class conflict and its adaptation by Lenin. Lenin had held that socialism could best be brought about through the efforts of a small, but dedicated and disciplined group acting in the name of the entire working class. The other is fascism, which is a less coherent ideology than communism, and may be viewed as a manifestation of extreme, irrational nationalism. It strives to achieve national unity and purpose by submerging and subordinating class differences and conflicts. Both communism and fascism are built around a totalitarian political party which attempts to permeate every aspect of the individual's life—cultural, religious, economic, and political.

Even before World War I had ended, Lenin's Bolshevik party in Russia overthrew the liberal-oriented but weak government of Kerensky and established in its place a totalitarian Communist dictatorship. In Italy, Benito Mussolini, in 1922, founded the first Fascist totalitarian regime by displacing a similarly weak and discredited liberal government. Immediately after World War I, a Fascist movement, Nazism, developed in Germany under Adolph Hitler, and on the wave of the despair and distress caused by the great depression of 1929, Germany's first liberal government fell to the Nazis.

Just as the establishment of a Communist regime in mighty Russia caused Communist parties to spring up in many countries, so also the establishment of a Fascist regime in powerful Germany inspired the formation of Fascist parties throughout the world. In Spain, a Fascist party called the *Falange* developed, and under the leadership of General Francisco Franco, overthrew Spain's floundering liberal government.

Franco's Fascist regime, built ostensibly around the Falange party, has been the undisputed government of Spain since 1939. Curiously, Franco, the weakest and least representative of the Fascist dictators, is the only European Fascist who is still in power. Franco's regime, although totalitarian in form like Nazi Germany or the Soviet Union, is in actuality much more akin to the simple military dictatorships which have existed throughout history where the main foundation of the regime lies in the army, rather than on a totalitarian party permeating the entire society. Although Franco's power is based on the organization of the Falange, two other organized groups, the army and the church, have also provided him with vital support.

Franco came to power through the savage and bitter civil war which devastated Spain from 1936-1939. To his credit he has given Spain peace and order, but he has not solved Spain's underlying social and economic problems. Indeed, he has aggravated many of them. He has enforced his will by means of a police state whose only mitigating feature is its inefficiency. His rule has been characterized by corruption and waste, very much like that of Farouk in Egypt, and Peron in Argentina.

Franco was born in 1892, and graduated from the famous military academy at Toledo at the age of eighteen. He served much of his early military career in Spanish Morocco. He was, like most other Spanish army officers, strongly anti-liberal, favoring the traditionalist right-wing parties. The Spanish army, like the armies in many Latin American countries, has long been involved in internal politics. In 1928, Franco became director of the military academy at Saragossa, but in 1931, Spain's new liberal government banished him from this position and closed the academy, which had become a hot-bed of anti-liberal agitation.

Franco returned to politics in 1933, when the elections of that year returned a right-wing government to power. Leading Arab troops from Morocco, he aided in suppressing a nationwide strike protesting the rightist regime. In 1935 he served briefly as minister of war and was established as a leading figure on the Spanish political scene. In February, 1936, a new liberal government came to power, which frightened many of the traditionalist elements in Spanish society. General Franco was one of a number of Army commanders who revolted against this government, and by July, 1936, he had become the military and civilian leader of the revolt.

The immediate cause of the Spanish Civil War was the refusal of the traditionalist elements in Spain to accept a modest but long overdue reform program announced by the liberal government. In the area of church-state relations, the liberals went too far. They pressed for wide-scale separation of church and state, without carefully considering the political consequences or having the strength to implement their program. Their leadership was made up largely of intellectuals inspired by the liberal ideas of the French Revolution but with too few practical politicians. They were also in disagreement on immediate and long-range policy objectives. The Spanish socialists' refusal to join with the liberal government also greatly weakened it.

The long-range causes of the Spanish Civil War were the country's sharp economic, social, and regional cleavages aggravated by the great depression. The reactionary, feudalistic nobility and landowning class were separated from, and indifferent to, the plight of the common people; in few Europeon countries was the difference of income between rich and poor so pronounced. In spite of her great past, Spain had dramatically declined in modern times and was far behind the rest of Western Europe agriculturally and industrially. These economic ills were at the root of Spain's long political instability, which in the 20th century was further provoked by the growing radicalism of her small, but badly exploited, industrial working class.

Spain has also been deeply divided by regional differences. Two of her most distinctive regions are Catalonia in the northeast, centered around Barcelona, and the Basque country in the north, both of whose populations, by language and tradition, feel themselves separate nationalities. For many hundreds of years, the national government in Madrid has sought to suppress the separatist tendencies in these regions. The problem is further aggravated by the fact that the Catalans and the Basques are more industrious and prosperous than other Spaniards. Understandably, these two regions were in the vanguard of opposition to General Franco and his rightist followers in the civil war, and have remained the regions most hostile to Franco's regime since 1939.

Before 1936, the Falange was politically insignificant. In the climate of fear and confusion which existed in Spain on the eve of the civil war, however, the Falange greatly increased its following. Franco, himself, though not at first a member of the Falange, recognized its usefulness, and very early in the civil war became its leader, consolidating other rightist elements into its ranks. In July, 1939, the victorious Franco made Spain a one-party state on the German and Italian model. In theory today, the Falange is a state within a state, with its own organization, military formations, and rigid code of discipline. Like other political institutions in Spain, however, the Falange is in reality poorly organized, and most of its local chapters and cells are little more than paper organizations, even though its membership totals over two hundred thousand. However, it has maintained the hierarchical Fascist party structure, with uniforms, the Fascist salute, and elaborate religious-like ceremonies, and has sought to advance the extreme goals of the Spanish nationalists.

Unlike the Fascist parties of Germany and Italy, the Spanish Falange never adopted an anti-church attitude, in part because of the deep religiosity of the Spanish people, and in part because of the historic subordination of the Spanish church to the national government—especially in regard to the appointment of bishops. The main theme of the Falange, as with all other Fascist parties, has been anti-communism and anti-socialism. Fascists have opposed these groups not because of the Communist and Socialist wish to nationalize property, but because of their emphasis on internationalism and class conflict, which the Fascists allege is unpatriotic and destructive of the unity of the nation. During times when people fear a Red menace, and fear that a liberal parliamentary government may be "too soft" on the Reds, Fascist parties attract their greatest support. Such was the case in Spain in 1936-37.

Spain is still smarting under the spiritual and physical wounds inflicted by its civil war. Coming from Spanish Morocco with a large force of Arab troops, Franco would have won the war in its opening months, but for a sizable part of the population, especially in the northern industrialized Basque and Catalan regions, that rallied to the government's side and succeeded in halting the rapid advance of the better organized and better equipped professional army forces of the rebels. Spain's militant trade union organizations and her Socialist and Communist parties also joined with the liberal government leaders. These labor groups soon came to be the organizational backbone of the government's forces, and they quickly assumed the leadership of the Loyalist side.

The civil war was fought with unbelievable ferocity. Fatalities exceeded the million mark. Both sides treated their prisoners cruelly, and disregarded the rights of the civilian population. Falangist gangs were particularly aggressive in attacking and killing Loyalist supporters. Because many Loyalists were militantly anticlerical, and because a large part of the Spanish church hierarchy supported the rebels, the conflict took on the color and fanaticism of a religious war.

Because they were fearful that the Spanish Civil War would turn into a world war, the major European nations agreed not to aid either the Loyalists or the rebels. Fascist Germany and Italy, and the Soviet Union, however, ignored the arms embargo and actively intervened in the war. Germany and Italy gave extensive financial and military aid to Franco, and thousands of professional troops from these countries served with the rebels. The Germans for their part welcomed this opportunity to apply and perfect many of their new military weapons and tactics—which they would use even more tellingly at a later date. Soviet Russia was the only important foreign supporter of the Loyalists, but aid from that source was negligible compared with the Fascist reinforcements. Communist parties throughout the world recruited volunteer units to fight Franco, of which the Abraham Lincoln Brigade from the United States was an example. As the war dragged on, the Communists in Spain, because of their dedication and discipline, assumed the leadership of the Loyalist side. Despite this the Loyalist cause received the ardent support of liberal public opinion everywhere. The war fired the hatred of liberals against Fascism and prepared many people emotionally for the impending struggle with Hitlerism. The legacy of the anti-Fascist sentiment engendered in the Spanish Civil War still causes important figures in Britain, France, and the United States to loathe the present Franco regime.

After consolidating his victory in 1939, Franco copied his senior Fascist partners by giving himself the title *Caudillo,* the Leader. He was astute enough to recognize that Spain could not involve herself actively in the struggle for Europe, and when World War II actually broke out, Franco declared Spain's neutrality. A large part of his officer corps, and much of the Falangist leadership pressed him to share the spoils of Europe with Hitler and Mussolini, but he refused. However, in the early stages of the war he warmly hailed Hitler's triumphs, and gave the Nazis extensive privileges in Spain, although never coming out openly for the Axis. He also supplied Hitler with a divison of troops to fight against the Soviet Union. As the Allies gained in strength against Hitler, however, Franco saw the writing on the wall and started to curry favor with the Allies. Following the Allied victory, he sought to join the United Nations; but Spain was refused membership in the UN, which denounced the Franco regime as a potential threat to world peace. The British and French governments even called upon the Spanish people to revolt against Franco and establish a truly democratic government.

Franco and his Falangist party had continually emphasized the anti-Communist character of their state. After the cold war began in 1947, and particularly after the outbreak of the Korean War in 1950, the Western Allies, somewhat reluctantly, began to take a more tolerant attitude toward Franco. The United States extended Marshall Plan aid to Spain in 1951, and since 1953 we have given

her over a billion dollars in military and economic aid. The UN also has opened its doors to Franco, admitting Spain as a member in 1955. However, the main Western military alliance, NATO, has refused to admit Franco Spain because of the strong anti-Franco sentiment among many liberal leaders of the NATO nations.

Until the summer of 1959, Franco tried to maintain rigid control over the Spanish economy. Following the example of Fascist Italy, he established so-called syndicates in the main professions and industries. These syndicates, in theory, represent the interests of the different labor and management groups, but are actually instruments of state control. Also following the Italian model, Franco established corporations, which in Spain are government agencies charged with supervising and aiding key private industries. These syndicates and corporations, although extremely corrupt, inefficient, and highly bureaucratic do make the state a partner in much of the country's industry.

To his credit, Franco has greatly reduced the perennial poverty of Spain, and has appreciably cut down unemployment, probably as a result of his policy of annually drafting large numbers of men into the army. He has carried out large-scale reforestation and reclamation projects in the arid mountain and plateau regions. Most important, he has taken significant, if costly steps toward industrializing Spain. Under him, a sizable middle class has emerged, made up of small businessmen and professionals, which may yet be the basis for a future democratic government. The cities of Spain reflect the growth of prosperity in this new middle class. Madrid has doubled in size since the war and boasts a number of ultra-modern apartment houses and new factories. In 1945 no one in Spain except the very rich had automobiles; today there are over six hundred thousand motor vehicles on the highways.

This surface prosperity partially conceals the fundamental weaknesses of Spain's economic system. The outward prosperity has been achieved by a ruinous inflation, and by other unsound economic practices which have brought Spain to the brink of bankruptcy. Until 1951 Franco followed a deflationary economic policy and did not encourage industrialization. Perhaps because of the great success of the Marshall Plan in re-establishing heavy industry in Western Europe, Franco launched a large-scale program,

still in progress, of building factories, shipyards, and transportation facilities. However, this new industrial economy is fundamentally unsound. The new industries are generally so inefficiently managed that they cannot compete with similar enterprises in Western Europe and must be subsidized by the government. Much of Spain's industry is monopolistic, with little or no competition, firms generally achieving a monopoly through favoritism and bribery, rather than through efficiency.

Perhaps the most serious consequence of his industrialization has been inflation. In recent years, prices in Spain have gone up over 15 per cent annually. The cost of living today is about *twenty* times what it was prior to the great depression. A large part of Spain's working population, her professional class, and even much of her officer corps, have had to take second jobs in order to survive. Workers in Spain have to work four times as long as workers in Great Britain to buy equivalent goods. This inflation, more than anything else, has greatly antagonized most of the Spanish population against Franco.

The characteristic that differentiates Franco from other totalitarian dictators is that he does not have the nucleus of dedicated and competent followers around which to build a modern state. The key men surrounding Franco are mainly concerned with furthering their own selfish interests. It is well known, for example, that Spain's ranking generals and members of Franco's own family —the inner group governing the country—have deposited hundreds of millions of dollars in foreign banks, particularly in Switzerland, and are parasitically attached to the system of graft and bribery which underlies Spain's present economic system. Smuggling is a major Spanish business, and the whole system of monopoly and controlled prices and wages encourages dishonesty. Spain's leaders show the kind of narrow outlook and greed which characterized Batista's and Peron's military dictatorships in Latin America.

Franco has also seriously neglected the problems of the mass of Spaniards on the land, although industrialization has absorbed some of the rural unemployed. Most Spanish farmers are desperately poor, and struggle with an arid, mountainous terrain, using primitive methods of farming. Moreover, they are still frequently op-

pressed by the landowning class.   Although most of Spain is still rural, a large part of her agricultural needs must now be imported.

In July 1959, under American and Western European pressure, Franco agreed to reverse his economic policies, and to introduce a liberal, or free economy in Spain. He has made a number of moves aimed at removing some of the more ponderous state controls. He has even talked of introducing a so-called "people's capitalism," under which workers could take out low-interest loans to buy a share in the industry in which they work.

If Franco were able to liberalize the Spanish economy, Spain would be enabled to end her economic isolation and become an integral part of Western Europe, perhaps through the Common Market. It is highly doubtful, however, that Franco's regime has the capacity or the intent to do this; more likely this new program is another device to persuade the representatives of the U.S. taxpayer to further subsidize Franco's dictatorship. It is debatable whether the huge American air bases in Spain are worth the loss of prestige that the United States suffers in propping up this backward and discredited dictator.

Every sign from Spain indicates that Franco and his Fascist Party, the Falange, have lost the support of all the important segments of the nation, including the army. The billion dollars in American aid, largely wasted, have enabled Franco to avoid his inevitable day of reckoning. His repeated boasts that his regime is the vanguard against communism are pathetic, untrue, and even humorous. Franco Spain is the personification of the greedy, parochial, and monopolistic order which Marx predicted was developing in Europe and which the Soviet propagandists wrongly charge exists among the Western democracies. People in many underdeveloped countries, including Spain, cannot help but be disillusioned by the contradictions between our professed goals and our actions. While we should not, of course, intervene in internal Spanish affairs, we should more carefully consider the wisdom of extending broad military and financial support to such dictators as Franco, who openly express their contempt for democratic government and individual freedom.

Spain cannot become a democracy overnight, but there is a strong and moderate non-Communist sentiment in the country

which could, on Franco's fall, provide the steppingstone to a more liberal and democratic Spain. The outlook for the future of Spain is considerably brighter now, therefore, than at many other periods in her history. Still, it is difficult to imagine any real or rapid progress in that country before the downfall of the man who now holds the reins of power—Francisco Franco.

V TITO OF YUGOSLAVIA: COMMUNIST NATIONAL STYLE

Immanuel Kant's famous saying that men should be treated as ends and not as means was carried over into modern politics by the German social democratic theorist, Edward Bernstein. Bernstein formulated the so-called revisionist critique of Marxism, which challenged Marx's basic assumption that the working class in liberal, industrialized states would be increasingly exploited by the capitalist class and that a working class or proletarian revolution would be inevitable. He denied Marx's doctrinaire view that capitalist society, guided by the irrevocable logic of history, would, of necessity, destroy itself. Bernstein contended that the rights of the working people could be achieved in many countries by evolutionary, or peaceful means, rather than by revolution. He urged socialists to concern themselves with practical goals, such as obtaining more favorable wages and hours, or improving working conditions. In the Kantian tradition he advised that the way in which socialists went about achieving their goals was all-important, and that the ultimate theoretical objective—a socialistic society—was insignificant; or, as Bernstein put it, "The movement is everything, the end is nothing."

In the countries of Western Europe, Bernstein's moderate revisionist approach has been accepted by the leading socialist parties, which today use parliamentary democratic procedures, de-emphasize class struggle, and reject revolution as a means for obtaining power.

However, in Russia the left, or Bolshevik, wing of the Socialist Party, under the leadership of Lenin, came to power in 1917 and established the present-day international Communist movement. Lenin accepted Marx's basic assumptions of class struggle and inevitable revolution, but he added to them the vanguard theory, that is, that the working class would come to power through the efforts of an elite, disciplined group, which ultimately would establish a classless society where the workers would have full power.

Since Lenin's time, Communist parties outside the Soviet Union have been marked by their complete subservience in matters of ideology and policy to the Soviet Communist Party. Stalin, Lenin's successor, made the international Communist movement his private instrument for advancing his personal views and the national interests of the Soviet Union.

Marshall Tito, Communist dictator of Yugoslavia, deserves examination for two reasons. He is the undisputed leader of his nation and controls its government and army with an iron hand. He rules his strategically located country through a totalitarian party basically the same as the Communist Party in the Soviet Union. Most important, though, Tito is the symbol of a new and heretical political ideology—national communism—the most disruptive force within international communism. Titoism has become synonymous with the doctrine of "separate roads to socialism," which has become the rallying cry of people in the Soviet satellites and of others who want to free themselves from Soviet domination, and who wish to have their countries follow their own national interests, rather than subordinate their interests to those of the Kremlin.

Tito's Yugoslavia, among the Communist nations, has pioneered in recognizing the importance of individual rights as opposed to those of the state. He has made fundamental modifications of the doctrinaire Marxist-Leninist approach by liberalizing the totalitarian economic and cultural controls of Yugoslavian life and allowing a major part of national production to be directed toward consumer goods rather than toward increasing the economic power of the state. To liberalize and humanize communism, and to relieve the people of the constant demands that they continually sacrifice themselves for the glory of the state are aims most evident in the satellite countries of Eastern Europe. These are also strongly present, though, among the citizens of the Soviet Union itself. The present Soviet leadership under Khrushchev has already made major concessions to Titoist ideas.

The international Communist movement is today in the throes

Josip Broz Tito: *"We have never given anybody reason to hope that we would join the Western bloc, or any other bloc for that matter. Our foreign policy is based on the clearly expressed principle of coexistence, on peaceful and equal cooperation with all countries, small or large."*

of a great idealogical struggle. On one side is the Stalinist view that all human and economic resources must be mobilized for the success and expansion of the Communist system. Red China is the most forceful representative of this school. On the other side is the Titoist view that there be some relaxation of control over the country's economic and political life, and that a more pragmatic approach be adopted. Titoism rejects the Stalinist conviction that war between the Western and Soviet blocs is inevitable. Although this struggle among leading Communists throughout the world was clearly not caused by Tito alone, there can be no doubt that Titoism has done more to mitigate the totalitarian character of the Communist system than all of America's propaganda efforts.

Titoism is an outgrowth of both the distinctive development of Yugoslavia and of the personality of Tito. Located in southeastern Europe, Yugoslavia, meaning "land of the southern Slavs," is the largest of the Balkan nations, having a population of 17 million. It is divided into several different religious and language groups. About 45% are of the Orthodox Christian faith; 35% are Roman Catholics, and 15% are Moslems. The most numerous, and for a long time, the most influential group in Yugoslavia has been the Serbs, who number over 7 million and are Orthodox Christians. Next in importance, and in many ways the most culturally and economically advanced are the Roman Catholic Croats, who number about 4 million. The Catholic Slovenes and the Orthodox Macedonians, are the two other groups of importance, each making up over a million of the population. Through the centuries, jealousies and hatreds between the different national groups developed in this area, the most intense animosity existing between the Orthodox Serbs and the Catholic Croats.

In the 19th and 20th centuries, Yugoslavia, long ruled by the old Austro-Hungarian and Ottoman Turkish Empires, was the tinderbox of Europe. It was the assassination of the Austrian archduke by a Serbian nationalist that sparked World War I. Because of the separate nationalist feelings of its people, Tito's Yugoslavia is federal in structure, with six member states.

Yugoslavia is a rocky and mountainous country. Although most of its people are still farmers, the fertility level of the soil is generally low. In spite of the major effort to industrialize under

Tito, most of the nation is still basically underdeveloped and backward. It has only a few big cities. Belgrade, the capital, with a population of half a million, is the largest.

Yugoslavia was created as a monarchy in 1919 by the Treaty of Versailles, largely from territory of the Austro-Hungarian Empire. Although the desire for unity of the Slavic peoples in the Balkans was partially fulfilled by the creation of the new country, the interwar history of the new nation was marked by bitterness and antagonisms among its different national groups. When the Nazis in World War II swept into the Balkans and conquered Yugoslavia, they had little difficulty in playing off one Yugoslav nationality against the other and further aggravating the bitterness between the different groups.

Tito was born in 1892 of a poor Croat family. He served in the Austrian army during World War I until captured by the Russians in 1915. In 1917, he joined the Red Army in Russia and served in it until 1920. He then returned to Yugoslavia, a convinced Communist, and gradually became the leading figure in the small underground Communist Party. He was one of the organizers and ranking commissars of the International Brigade which fought Franco in Spain. He also spent several years in the Soviet Union during Stalin's purges of the late 1930's and, according to his own later statement, was himself almost purged by the suspicious dictator.

When World War II broke out Tito returned to Yugoslavia and led the underground Communist resistance to the Nazis. In Yugoslavia, as in other occupied nations such as Italy and France, the Communists emerged as the most daring and determined fighters against the Germans. In the mountainous terrain of Yugoslavia, Tito was able to weld together a closely-knit and formidable fighting force. Although he was often unscrupulous and cruel in his dealings with the non-Communist opponents of the Nazis, he was able to hold a sizable part of Yugoslavia even during the Nazi occupation and was clearly the master of the country when the Nazi power declined.

It was during the war years that Tito showed the remarkable independence of spirit and arrogant self-confidence that have so marked his personality as leader of Yugoslavia. British, American, and even Soviet officials who dealt with him during the war found him to be shrewd and intelligent, unafraid of discussing even the most controversial issues. When the war ended, a republic was proclaimed and Tito became its head.

Prior to 1948 Tito was a loyal and obedient Communist and he dutifully established in Yugoslavia a Communist satellite regime, accepting without question the guidance and example of the Soviet Union. However, in one respect he was unique among the post-war satellite leaders. All of them (with the exception of the Czechs, who were not brought into the Communist fold until later) had had their countries liberated by the victorious Red Army of the Soviet Union. Tito, however, had liberated his country with his own forces, and owed the Soviets no debt on this score.

Tito proceeded to transform Yugoslavia into a single-party totalitarian dictatorship, modeled on the Soviet Union and the other satellites. His all-powerful Communist Party rapidly extended its influence throughout the country. Mass meetings and rallies, in the totalitarian fashion, are frequently held to encourage and incite the population to support government policies and to meet production quotas. Tito is frequently the central figure at these demonstrations. Dressed often in his marshal's uniform, he speaks to the people in one or all of the three official languages of Yugoslavia. All the propaganda media—radio, newspapers, billboards, and motion pictures—are mobilized to glorify the party state and to advertise its goals. Through the schools and the country's extensive youth organizations, the party constantly tries to mold the youth of Yugoslavia in its own image.

From 1945 to 1948 Tito became increasingly dissatisfied with Stalin's arbitrary rule of the Communist world. He resented having to subordinate Yugoslavia's interests to those of the Soviet Union. He wanted Yugoslavia to industrialize rapidly, but Stalin wished to make it primarily a supplier of raw materials for the Soviet orbit. The cult of Stalin's personality was reaching its high point at this time. Communists within and outside the Soviet Union were compelled to idolize and extol the old dictator to an absurd degree. Stalin was growing increasingly suspicious of anyone who showed the slightest independence of judgment.

Finally, in June 1948, Yugoslavia was expelled from the

Cominform, the international Communist body, and thereupon the Communist world proceeded to denounce Tito. The Soviet Union and its satellites broke off all economic and cultural relations with him and began to threaten military action. Tito found that he was almost completely surrounded by hostile Communist neighbors—Hungary, Rumania, Bulgaria and Albania. However, an embargo and savage propaganda attacks failed to shake the loyalty of the Yugoslav Army and Communist Party to Tito. Moreover, many non-Communist Yugoslavs, who disliked Tito, feared and hated the Soviet Union even more and rallied to his support. Nationalism became the main ingredient in Titoism—hence the term National Communism. In the Communist satellites today, Titoism has been the rallying cry of those who wish to put their own national interests—Polish, Hungarian, Rumanian—before the interests of the Soviet Union.

Lashing back at the Stalinists, Tito has continually maintained that his is a socialist regime. He argues that revolution is often necessary to transform a feudal backward state into a socialist one; but denounces the Soviets' blind adherence to revolutionary dogma. He has also criticized the cruel political system which Stalin created in the Soviet Union and imposed on the satellite peoples.

Tito's strong opposition to the Soviet Union soon won him extensive aid from the United States and its allies. Since 1950, the United States has given Tito a billion dollars in aid, about half in the form of surplus food and half for economic and military development. This support has enabled Yugoslavia to defend itself and to develop its economic potential. Tito, in return, has permitted greater freedom in Yugoslavia but has insisted that he will not be a member of either the Eastern or Western bloc. The United States has wisely refrained from insisting that Tito join the West as a condition for economic support and is content merely that Yugoslavia stay out of the Soviet bloc. Yugoslavia is classed with the so-called "neutralist" nations, including India, Indonesia and Ceylon, which refuse to join either the East or the West in the Cold War. Our government feels that even though "neutralist" nations, such as India or Yugoslavia, often side with Moscow and criticize our policies, their existence as independent and strong nations is a vital bulwark of our security.

From 1948 onwards, those persons in the satellite countries who favored more moderate policies, and a lessening of Soviet control, came to be called Titoists. During his lifetime, Stalin regularly persecuted and jailed such persons.

In 1953, Stalin died, and his successor proceeded to loosen many of the hated totalitarian controls binding the Soviet people and the satellite nations. A thaw in Soviet-Yugoslav relations developed, culminating in the famous "pilgrimage" to Yugoslavia in May, 1955, of the top Soviet leaders, led by Khrushchev. They, in effect, apologized for past policies and blamed Stalin's secret police chief, Beria, for much of the misunderstanding. During this visit, the Soviet leaders agreed to recognize Yugoslavia as an equal. Tito's greatest triumph, however, was the acceptance by the Soviet Union of three main principles of Titoism; that there are separate roads to socialism, that war is not inevitable, and that revolutionary action is not always necessary to socialize a nation. The understandings reached in this 1955 meeting were, temporarily at least, made official Communist dogma at the celebrated 20th Party Congress in Moscow in February, 1956, called by some the "Titoist Congress." At this gathering Khrushchev made his famous denunciation of Stalin and of many of Stalin's methods. More important from Tito's point of view, however, was the acknowledgement that the Kremlin had no monopoly on socialism and that relations between communist states should be "equal, frank and free."

The "thaw" in general Soviet policy over the years 1953 to 1956 was paralleled by friendly relations between Tito and the Kremlin. Yugoslavia again began to receive economic aid from the Soviets and resumed commercial and political relations with the satellite countries. When the Soviet Union began to harden its policy line after 1956, Tito and Titoism again became the subjects of sharp Soviet attacks. In the satellite empire, the "thaw" encouraged the expression of pent-up popular resentment against Communist "puppet" rulers.

In 1956, revolts broke out against the Communist regimes in Poland and Hungary. The Poles, more prudent perhaps than the Hungarians, did not insist on the complete dissolution of ties with the Soviet system, but limited their demands to a greater degree of independence from Moscow and greater freedom from party control. Wladyslaw Gomulka, previously jailed and condemned by Stalin as a Titoist, has emerged as the leader of this new Poland. The United States tacitly supports Gomulka by giving Poland large amounts of surplus foods. The Hungarian Revolt was also led by many people influenced by Titoism, but responding to their people's ardent desire for freedom from Moscow, they sought to take Hungary out of the Soviet system and make it "neutralist." This the Kremlin would not allow and the Soviet army brutally crushed the revolt.

Since that time Soviet-Yugoslav relations have been tense but not as strained as they were during the Stalin period. In all the satellite countries, Tito remains the symbol of the desire for greater freedom. In announcing the execution of Imre Nagy, Titoist leader of the Hungarian revolt, the Communists charged that Tito had inspired the revolution. Nagy, interestingly, had fled to the Yugoslav Embassy, but was lured out by a safe-conduct agreement and then betrayed. His assassination was clearly meant to serve as a warning to other Titoists behind the Iron Curtain.

By the end of 1957, the Soviet Union reneged on its promises, stopped economic aid to Yugoslavia and resumed its attacks upon Titoism as a form of "revisionism." Tito, well aware that he is practically surrounded by the Soviet bloc, has been comparatively moderate in answering these attacks. He has held fast to the "neutralist" argument that the Eastern and Western blocs are equally wrong and that both menace the existence of mankind.

Tito has continued to try to influence and woo the satellite leaders, especially Gomulka of Poland. In September, 1957, Gomulka visited Yugoslavia as Tito's guest and the two men issued a statement which declared that "our countries are building socialism, each in its own way, and according to its own conditions." Gomulka has been forced to follow the general Soviet propaganda line regarding the Titoist heresy, but there is no question that the actual government of Poland is based on Titoist principles.

In the Communist world, the most rabid Stalinists are the Red Chinese leaders. Calling the Yugoslavs "fascists," "tools of capitalism," and "traitors to socialism," they have refused dealings of any sort with Yugoslavia. In the current dispute between Peiping and

Moscow, the Stalinist-Titoist roots of the struggle are apparent. Tito was for a time hopeful that Khrushchev would remove from communism its Stalinist character.

Tito is performing an important service to the West by helping the "neutralist" nations understand and resist the blandishments of the Kremlin. He carries on extensive correspondence and holds frequent meetings with such leaders as Sukarno of Indonesia, Nehru of India and Nasser of Egypt. It is thought that Tito is warning these men of the dangers of flirting too intimately with Moscow. Moreover Soviet unwillingness to honor its aid agreements with Yugoslavia when Tito refused to knuckle under to Russia has made a great impression on the "neutralist" leaders whose basic desire is to steer a middle course between Moscow and Washington.

Although Tito has held many meetings with Nasser and often supports the Egyptian ruler's demands for Arab independence and for non-intervention by the great powers in the Middle East, he has criticized Nasser's so-called "positive neutralism"—the policy of playing off the West against the East to gain economic and political advantages. Tito feels that Nasser may be playing with fire and unwittingly increasing world tension and the danger of nuclear war.

Tito has also worked hard to secure the Balkans against foreign intervention. Although he is critical of NATO, nevertheless, in a 1954 mutual defense agreement he aligned himself with two NATO members, Turkey and Greece. With Greece, especially, Tito has made great efforts to restore friendly relations.

We of the West, although recognizing the dictatorial character of Tito's regime, should continue to encourage democratic developments within Communist Yugoslavia. In our support of Yugoslavia, we are primarily concerned with protecting ourselves against Soviet expansion. Furthermore, there is every reason to hope that the concessions to liberalism that Tito has made will undermine and ultimately destroy the totalitarian character of his government.

VI KEMAL ATATURK: MODERNIZER OF TURKEY

In May, 1960 Turkey seeemed to take a step backward from parliamentary democracy when the army officer corps carried out a bloodless coup. A group of ranking officers, calling themselves the Committee of National Unity, led by General Cemal Gursel, took over the effective leadership of the nation. General Gursel has pledged that military rule is only provisional and that a new constitution with free elections will soon re-establish civilian government. He has, however, filled the jails with leaders of the old regime, many of whom will face trial for treason, and he has effectively disbanded the Democratic Party which had been governing Turkey for the previous ten years. Turkey's still hopeful outlook for the future and her general political stability have been brought about by the work of one man—Mustapha Kemal, known as Ataturk.

General Gursel justified the take-over by saying that "we resorted to action in order to re-open the path blazed by Ataturk, when it was about to be blocked." This view seems to have been shared by the overwhelming majority of Turkish nationalists, both in the civilian population and in the army, who came to feel that the dominant Democratic Party had turned its back on the policies of Turkey's greatest national figure.

Almost singlehandedly, Ataturk changed Turkey into a reasonably modern national state modeled on the nations of Western Europe. Although he was a dictator, his goal was democracy, and he succeeded in inspiring the entire educated class with his idealism. Under Ataturk's guidance, Turkey turned her back on the conquest of other nationalities and concentrated her energies on educating and Westernizing her backward population and raising the standard of living. Ataturk had an uncanny ability to know how far he could push his people to change their ways. He recognized that it would take several generations to complete many of the reforms he had inaugurated.

The Republic of Turkey has an area of 300,000 square miles, somewhat larger than Texas. Most Turks are employed in agriculture and live in thousands of small villages scattered across the vast plateau regions and valleys of the country. Over 25 million people live in Turkey today, the population having doubled in less than 30 years.

The Turks were the dominant nationality in the Ottoman Empire which ruled the middle east and much of southeastern Europe for 400 years prior to 1914. However, by the year 1800 the countries of Western Europe with their technological know-how and their more modern social and political institutions, had become far more powerful, both militarily and economically than the backward, feudalistic Ottomans. The Ottoman Empire existed throughout the 19th century as a buffer state and was little more than a protectorate of the great European powers.

In 1908, a Turkish nationalist group—known as the Young Turks—made up of Western-educated intellectuals and army officers, seized power from the Ottoman caliph. They were disgusted at the military weakness and corruption of the regime and wished to restore the dignity and power of the Turkish nation.

The Young Turks were little different from other nationalist groups that were so active throughout central and southern Europe in the 19th century. Unfortunately, the Young Turk regime was soon drawn into war with other nationalities in the Balkans, and in 1914 Turkey entered World War I on the side of Germany. The end of the war found much of Turkey's territory occupied by the British, French, Italians and Greeks; the country was in ruins and national morale was at a low ebb. It was then that Ataturk took command of his nation's destiny and changed the course of its history.

Ataturk was born in 1880, the son of a Turkish government official in the Balkan city of Salonika, in the European part of Ottoman Turkey. He was brought up in a military atmosphere and like many middle-class Turks living in the Balkans, he entered

Mustapha Kemal Ataturk: "*. . . Let the people leave politics alone for the present. Let them interest themselves in agriculture and commerce. For ten years more I must rule. After that I may be able to let them speak openly.*"

a military academy while still in his teens. In 1904, he graduated from the staff college in Constantinople and was established as a prominent and able professional soldier. With many other young officers he joined the secret Young Turk movement and played an important role in the revolt of 1908.

Although he was resentful of the German officers who attempted to dominate Turkey, Ataturk took a leading role in the military action of World War I. He was commander in the famous Gallipoli campaign in 1915, and his brilliant tactics there in repulsing the British made him famous. After the war, Ataturk, now a general, was given the position of inspector-general of Anatolia, the central highland region of Turkey. He was under orders to administer the armistice and disarm the population. Instead, he rallied together disbanded and demoralized army units and soon was in open defiance of the government in Constantinople. With ragged but determined troops, he proceeded to seize control of what is now Turkey. By 1921, he had defeated the Armenians in the East, and in 1922, his forces defeated a Greek army and had pushed across Turkey to the Mediterranean.

The British, who had occupied Constantinople and the Turkish Straits, were Ataturk's only remaining enemy—the Italians and the French having agreed to withdraw for economic and political concessions. For several weeks in September and October, 1922, it appeared that Turkey and Britain might again go to war, but the British government under Lloyd George backed down, and Ataturk became the complete master of his nation.

From 1922 until his death, Ataturk served as president, in reality dictator, of Turkey. The tremendous prestige and veneration he had earned as liberator of his country enabled him to introduce the changes that are revolutionizing Turkish life.

Perhaps the greatest legacy that Ataturk left his people was a tradition of moderate nationalism. Anti-foreign sentiment was intense in Turkey when Ataturk came to power. Wars of aggression in the Middle East or in the Balkans could easily have resulted from the Turks' long-standing feuds with neighboring nationalities. Under Ataturk, Turkey turned her back on imperialism and concentrated on the building of a strong national state. The Turks also rejected the idea of Pan Turanianism; that is, a union under their leadership of all the different Turkish peoples scattered through the Middle East and the Soviet Union. Ataturk inaugurated a policy of peaceful and friendly relations with neighboring states which the Turkish government has continuously followed since his time.

Although Ataturk was a dictator and often acted ruthlessly in suppressing opposition, he wanted his nation to be a progressive democratic state, similar to Britain or France, and an equal member of the European family of nations.

Supported by a large group of nationalists coming mainly from the Young Turk movement, he was able to direct the strong patriotic feelings among the Turkish masses along constructive lines.

Because he wanted his people to be nationalistic, not cosmopolitan or Levantine, he transferred the nation's capital from Constantinople to Ankara. Constantinople for thousands of years had been a great cosmopolitan center with many different nationalities, and Ataturk felt it had been a corrupting influence on past regimes. Ankara, in the Anatolian highlands, was a village in 1922; but it has grown into a great city of over a million people and is today Turkey's political center. However, Constantinople remains the cultural, and to a lesser extent, the economic center of the country.

Ataturk felt that the Moslem religion seriously retarded the emancipation of the Turkish people from traditional habits and customs. One of his first major political acts was to abolish the caliphate in 1923. For 500 years the sultan of Turkey had been the caliph or spiritual leader of the Moslem world. This had been a source of much pride and some power for the Turkish sultans. The creation of the Turkish Republic had already abolished the sultanate. Ataturk then formally separated church and state in Turkey and, to emphasize this separation, he changed the day of rest from the Moslem Friday to Sunday. To replace the religious law which had been in force in Turkey under the Ottomans, Ataturk substituted a modern legal system based largely on the civil code of Switzerland and the criminal law of Italy.

One of his most dramatic actions was to compel the Turks to abandon the fez and wear European style headgear. This was part of his drive to persuade Turks to dress in the Western manner.

Headgear in the Middle East has been traditionally a sign of social and religious position, and Ataturk's success in outlawing the fez marked an important psychological victory for him in Westernizing his country. The Moslem religion is still a great force among the rural masses of Turkey, but the growing educated class is militantly secular in outlook. One factor which, more than anything else, turned the educated element in Turkey against the Democratic Party in 1960 was the belief that it was making major concessions to the religious feelings of the masses, in defiance of the secular tradition left by Ataturk.

The women of present-day Turkey, perhaps more than any other group, have reason to be grateful to Ataturk. He had long believed that women should have complete social and political equality with men. His reforms had their greatest impact in changing the status of women. In the cities, and in many of the towns and villages, Turkish women today live much the same way and enjoy the same rights as do the women in any Western nation. Men in the traditional Moslem society have had unusual prerogatives in their relationship with their wives. Divorce could be had at the husband's whim, and a woman could be made one of four wives in a harem.

Modern Turkish women, who are renowned for their beauty, are playing important roles in the civil service and the professions. A higher percentage of Turkish women have graduated from secondary school and university than women in any other Moslem state.

Ataturk knew that the Turks would have to be educated before they could enjoy democracy. He directed much of his energies to building a national school system which would combat the almost universal illiteracy of his people. Today there are 20,000 public schools in Turkey and four first-rate universities. About half of the adult population can now read and write. Moreover, there are several hundred thousand high school and university graduates, who make up the intelligentsia and provide the educated nucleus so necessary for the Westernization of any underdeveloped nation.

Another reform Ataturk put through was to change the script used in writing the Turkish language. He substituted the Latin script for the traditional Arabic alphabet. This was a grave affront to devout Moslems, who looked upon Arabic as a holy script, but Ataturk was convinced that it was poorly suited to the Turkish language, and felt that this would be anoher way to tie Turkey to the West. He required that all Turkish newspapers be written in the Latin script, and he traveled across the country, urging and persuading his people to learn to read and write their language in Latin characters. Perhaps the most famous photograph of Ataturk is the one showing him at a blackboard teaching his people to write in the new way.

Ataturk ruled Turkey with the aid of a single political party, the Popular Republican Party, which became, in effect, the successor of the Young Turk movement. During his lifetime, advancement in the army or civil service was tied in with party membership. At one time, Ataturk experimented with a two-party system. He asked several leading supporters of his to form a loyal opposition in the Grand National Assembly, Turkey's parliament. So much bitterness and misunderstanding developed, however, that he soon reverted to the single-party system.

Ataturk introduced into Turkey a type of planned state economy which has been called *Etatism*. Under this policy, the Turkish state took the responsibility for the development of industry and most other major forms of economic activity, including banking and mining. Ataturk favored this because he feared that, otherwise, foreign investors would control the Turkish economy, and would call on the great powers to intervene in internal Turkish affairs to protect their interests and preserve their special privileges. There was also a great lack of private capital in Turkey, making more state investment a necessity. Turkey did not develop its economy rapidly until after 1947 and the coming of American economic aid.

Ismet Inonu, who had been Ataturk's principal lieutenant for many years, became President of Turkey in 1938 on the death of Ataturk. Inonu, following a policy of neutrality, guided Turkey safely through World War II. After the war, the Turks, fearful of the Soviet Union, allied themselves closely with the United States and participated in the formation of the North Atlantic Treaty Organization.

Till the end of 1949, Turkey remained a one-party dictatorship under Inonu. The growing democratic sentiment in Turkey, however, and the desire to show the world, especially the United States, that the nation was politically mature, caused Inonu and his supporters to allow a genuine opposition party to compete in the 1950 elections. The Democratic Party, which had been a faction within the Popular Republican ranks, was formed under the leadership of Celal Bayar, a veteran political figure. To the surprise of the world, the Democrats won a decisive victory in 1950, and Inonu stepped down and allowed Bayar to become president.

The Democratic victory in 1950 reflected the widespread dissatisfaction with the rigid political and economic controls of the previous regime. Not only had there been a huge bureaucracy to carry out the normal governmental functions, but also similar large government bureaucracies to operate Turkey's industry, public utilities and commercial activities. The Democrats had promised to liberalize the economy, lessen state controls and encourage the investment of foreign capital.

One group that gave the Democrats strong support was the farmers. Turkey's poor and backward agricultural class had largely been neglected in favor of the city and town dwellers by both Ataturk and Inonu. Ancient methods of farming are still generally used throughout most of Turkey, although American economic aid in 1947 introduced much mechanized farming equipment. U.S. technical aid missions also helped many thousands of Turkish farmers and greatly improved the quality and quantity of their crops. From 1951 to 1953 Turkey enjoyed successive record harvests, and for the first time the country became a major exporter of grains and cereals. These bumper crops were caused by unusually good weather and by the extensive mechanization of some of the larger farms. Serious droughts hit the country over the years 1954 through 1957 and Turkey was forced to import grains from the United States in order to feed her population. There have been serious problems in maintaining the modern farm equipment. Replacement parts have been expensive and much machinery has been ruined by improper upkeep. The Bayar government, in order to keep the support of the farmers, gave them extensive agricultural subsidies and tax concessions. However, combined with a too-ambitious program in support of industrial projects, especially sugar refineries and hydro-electric plants, this project caused a serious inflation to grip the country by 1956.

As the inflation grew worse, criticism of the Democratic Party and the Bayar government mounted. The government then reimposed many harsh, dictatorial restrictions on the rights of the opposition. Starting in 1954, the Bayar regime began to severely repress opposition newspapers, and even to prohibit public criticism of the government. Soon a large part of the educated class of Turkey came to lose confidence and faith in the Democratic Party. In the universities, in the army officer corps, and in the huge governmental bureaucracy there was widespread discontent. The Democratic leadership more and more depended on the support of the common people to counterbalance the opposition of the intellectual class. This was a main reason for the widespread religious and economic concessions which the regime made to the people. For example the permission to allow the call to prayer to be made in Arabic, rather than Turkish, greatly provoked nationalist sentiment.

The Bayar regime also, contrary to the tradition of Ataturk, attempted to incite violent anti-foreign and aggressive sentiment in Turkey over the issue of Cyprus. Ataturk had worked hard to restore friendship between Turks and Greeks, but the Bayer government, apparently to gain public support, fanned public resentment in Turkey over the treatment of the Turkish Cypriots. In 1955, encouraged by government propaganda, widescale looting and burning of Greek property worth hundreds of millions of dollars took place all over Turkey.

In the spring of 1960, however, the Democrats went too far. In preparation for the scheduled 1961 elections, a large-scale purge of the bureaucracy and the army officer corps was attempted, apparently in order that the pending elections could be successfully rigged. Tension mounted and university students, inspired by the success of South Korean students in overthrowing an unpopular government, rebelled against the regime. The Bayar government led by Premier Adman Menderes, attempted to impose martial law but the army leadership under Generel Gursel had had enough and they took command of the country.

In most other countries of the Middle East, this turn of events would mean a long period of military dictatorship and political upheaval. This probably will not be the case in Turkey, where the roots of democracy are strong, and where there is a remarkable agreement among the leaders as to what the nation's objectives should be.

VII BEN GURION OF ISRAEL: FATHER
OF A NEW NATION

David Ben Gurion, Prime Minister of Israel, is inspired by a burning sense of history, which has guided him since childhood. Like the Biblical prophets whom he so closely resembles, Ben Gurion is a mystic and a dreamer: but he is also a man of the world and a practical politician. Since his youth he has been a dedicated Labor-Zionist and has struggled to rebuild a national Jewish homeland. The emergence of Israel's elaborate welfare institutions and the dominance of her powerful trade unions are largely his handiwork. Although totally involved in the achievement and development of Jewish statehood, Ben Gurion is a man of universal interests, and has never limited his outlook to his own nation. He is an avid student of world history and is especially intrigued by Greek and Chinese philosophy. He envisions that Israel will never be a great political power, but that it will achieve its destiny as a spiritual center and model of new social and political forms for the emerging nations of Asia and Africa.

Ben Gurion has been the unchallenged leader of Israel since its creation, and governs through the largest labor party, the *Mapai*. Many newcomers to Israel have looked upon him as an heir of the ancient prophets, and their almost religious veneration of him has been a source of political strength.

David Ben Gurion was born David Green in a small Polish town in 1886. His father, Avigdor Green, was a lawyer and a modernist, who rebelled against the orthodoxy of the Polish ghetto. He was a leader of the group know as "The Lovers of Zion" which sought to revive Hebrew as a living language and to re-establish Jewish life in the Holy Land. When Theodore Herzl founded political Zionism in 1897, the Green home became a regular meeting place for Zionist gatherings At this time most of the country was ruled by the oppressive and bigoted Czarist Russian government, which increasingly persecuted Russia's minority nationalities, especially the Jews. Like many other young Jews, Ben Gurion identified himself with the labor movement, the main symbol of opposition to the Czar and of the struggle for political and economic freedom. At the age of fourteen, Ben Gurion helped form a Hebrew-speaking Zionist youth society in his native city, and he was soon traveling about Poland, speaking and organizing for Labor Zionism.

In 1906 he emigrated to Turkish Palestine, where for several years he worked as a farm laborer in small and backward Jewish agricultural villages. His flair for organizing and leadership soon became evident. Shortly after his arrival, he had helped found the Workers of Zion Party, which was to become the Mapai, and in 1910 he was appointed editor of Palestine's first labor newspaper in Jerusalem. He also helped establish the Jewish defense group which was to evolve into the Israeli army. While in Jerusalem, he decided to go to Turkey to study law so that he could aid the Palestine Jewish community in its relations with the Turks.

His studies in Constantinople were soon interrupted by the outbreak of World War I, and Ben Gurion and other prominent Palestinian Zionists were exiled by the Turks. He came to the United States in 1915 and worked with Zionist societies in this country. In 1918, he joined a specially formed Jewish legion within the British army and served with it in Egypt and Palestine. With the war's end Ben Gurion returned to Palestine and soon became the most prominent leader of the small but highly organized labor movement. In 1921 he became general secretary of the newly formed *Histadrut,* the General Confederation of Israeli Labor, which incorporated all of the splinter labor Zionist groups. The Histadrut, which is today controlled by the Mapai Party, is the main political power behind the Israeli government. Under Ben Gurion's leadership, the Histadrut early expanded its activities to include the management and ownership of industry. It has had the dual objectives of wishing to advance the interests of labor and of promoting the establishment of a Jewish state.

The Jewish immigrants who came to Palestine prior to 1933

David Ben Gurion: *"We will bring water to the desert. We will exploit every drop of water from the skies and from the ground. We will make the wasteland fruitful and turn it into a Garden of Eden. We will raze the slums and assure every citizen of a reasonable level of education, income, housing, and economic security throughout his life. We will build here an example to the world, and we will be truly a chosen people, without classes, without exploitation or discrimination, fulfilling the dreams of our prophets of old. . . ."*

were largely from Eastern Europe and were overwhelmingly pro-labor in sentiment. Most joined the labor parties affiliated with the Histadrut. After 1920, under the new British mandate, a provisional Jewish government developed, controlled from the beginning by the Histadrut parties. Ben Gurion, as leader of the Histadrut, emerged as the principal spokesman for the Palestine Jewish Community. Today, although a native-born generation is taking over the political leadership in Israel, the country's many political parties are still strongly East European in outlook. The Mapai corresponds to the moderate Social Democratic parties found throughout Europe.

Ben Gurion has been almost consistently an admirer of the British and of their system of government, having been especially impressed by Churchill's leadership during World War II. Had it not been for British interests in the Arab states, there is no question that Israel would today be a member of the British Commonwealth. By the late 1930's, as the Jewish situation in Europe became more imperiled, the British began to go back on their promises and to restrict Jewish settlement and land ownership in Palestine. Ben Gurion led the resistance to these policies, directing the smuggling of immigrants through the British blockade and the organization of the underground defense army. The most prominent Zionist leader outside of Israel was Chaim Weizmann, who was to become Israel's first president. He opposed Ben Gurion's activist policies against the British and placed his hopes on diplomatic negotiations.

By 1942, the world situation convinced Ben Gurion that Jewish statehood in Palestine was imperative, and he led the drive which culminated in Israel's independence in May, 1948, and the subsequent Jewish victory over the neighboring Arab states.

The new Israeli government was modeled closely on that of Great Britain, having a strong prime minister and a weak president. The prime minister and his cabinet are chosen by the Parliament, or *Knesset,* made up of 120 members. Because Israel has so many political parties, a simple form of proportional representation is used to elect members of the Knesset. The voter casts his ballot for one of a dozen or more slates of candidates, prepared by the parties, and each slate receives a number of seats corresponding to its percentage of the total vote. Mapai has consistently received about 35% of the vote, more than double that of any other party. It receives most cabinet positions, including prime minister, but it must rule in coalition with other parties.

Although the coalition governments that have ruled Israel since 1948 have been regularly strained by factional and ideological differences, the country's democratic institutions have remained intact. Ben Gurion's prestige and political skill have been a major factor contributing to the success of the Israeli government. Under him, Israel has more than doubled in population and has absorbed over a million immigrants, more than half of whom came from backward countries of Asia and Africa. Although most of them have had no tradition or experience with democratic government, they have been peacefully integrated into the political system created by the Eastern European founders of the state. The democratic character of Israel is all the more remarkable in view of the fact that the Arab threat has kept the country in a constant state of mobilization. Military preparedness has been the dominant factor in the government's thinking.

Ben Gurion has always proclaimed the virtues of pioneering in the Holy land. He calls upon Jewish youth in Israel and abroad to settle in the frontier or desert regions of the country in order to take part personally in draining the swamp and turning back the deserts. The young Jew, he has said, will achieve personal happiness and will strengthen himself as a person by rebuilding the Jews' ancestral homeland.

Inspired by both Zionist and socialist idealism, Ben Gurion and his contemporaries settled in Palestine as pioneers. They were determined to create a new and better society and to sink roots into the land by toil, sweat and blood. Women also came as pioneers and worked alongside the men.

Only a small percentage of Israeli youth have responded to Ben Gurion's appeal to devote their lives to pioneering, but large numbers do spend several years in special youth corps and scout groups in frontier settlements and in immigrant villages.

In 1953, Ben Gurion dramatized his views by retiring from the premiership and settling for fourteen months with his wife in a small collective village in Israel's southern Negev desert. Here he worked as an agricultural laborer, sharing with young pioneers the rigors of frontier life. He retired partly because he wished more time to meditate and read, but he also wanted to set an example to Israel's newcomers, especially the immigrant youth. He had long proclaimed the urgency of settling and building up the hot and dry Negev region, which makes up over half of Israel's territory, and he hoped that others would follow him. "For those who make the desert bloom," he said, "there is room for thousands, even millions. And the destiny of the state is in the hands of the many rather than of a single individual." Further stressing the importance of an intensified program of land development and afforestation, Ben Gurion stated:

> It is absolutely vital for the State of Israel, for both economic and security reasons, to move southwards: to direct the country's water and rain, the young pioneers and the new immigrants, and most of the resources of the Development Budget, to the south; to uproot a considerable proportion of our workshops and factories and transfer them to the south; to move a number of our scientific and research institutions, dealing with the country's geography, soil structure, vegetation, climate and natural resources, to the south. We must concentrate the attention of Israel's scientists and research workers on the investigation of the forces, whether known or latent, with whose assistance we shall be able to make the lands of the south and the Negev thrive and flourish.

Prior to 1948, the Jewish population of Israel was largely of European origin. The large number of Asian and African immigrants who have recently settled in the country have created a special social problem. Almost half of Israel's population is now of non-European background and can be described as colored. Many of them came diseased and illiterate, and almost all of them were unfamiliar with the Western way of life. They also had few skills which could easily be adapted to a modern industrialized nation.

Today the European Israelis tend to have the best jobs because of their superior educational background, whereas the colored Israelis work largely as unskilled laborers. The managerial and administrative class and the officer corps in the army are almost entirely European. This situation has, understandably, created resentment among the newcomers.

Ben Gurion has been very conscious of this problem and his government has made a determined effort to raise the standards of the colored immigrants. The army has conducted special courses to prepare such newcomers for skilled positions and leadership. The graduation several years ago of the first young immigrant from backward Yemen as a jet pilot was given wide publicity. Ben Gurion, who has had a special affection for the Yemenites, has said that the day that Israel inaugurates its first Yemenite prime minister will mark the end of this division of the country into two communities.

Ben Gurion's ability to adjust to new conditions has helped to make him an outstanding leader. Although he has never wavered in his determination to rebuild Zion, he has been willing to discard old ideas and revise political institutions as changing circumstances dictate. In 1952 over great opposition, he pushed through the reparations agreement with Germany which has provided Israel with almost a billion dollars in economic aid. Although many Israelis wanted no dealings with a nation which a few years before had murdered millions of their brethren, Ben Gurion argued that the country's duty was to support the living. And economic assistance was a necessity for the continued survival of the new nation.

Ben Gurion has also come to believe that his Mapai Party is out of step with the times. He has urged Israel's dominant labor party to reject the old East European class warfare slogans. In Israel, as in the United States, a majority of the wage earners work in non-productive white-collar occupations, and only a minority are in productive occupations such as farming. Since the white-collar employees do not usually regard themselves as being in the "working class," it became apparent that the party would have to broaden its appeal so as to gain the support of this group also. Ben Gurion has, in effect, been urging the Mapai to become a national party open to the managerial and middle classes as well as to labor; and that it be dedicated to social reform rather than merely to a socialist political ideology.

Ben Gurion's views were sharply criticized by Israel's other labor parties and by many members of Mapai itself. The Israeli general elections at the end of 1959, however, showed that a large part of Israel's voters agreed with Ben Gurion. Mapai increased its part of the total vote to almost 40 per cent and the other labor parties declined from 20 to 16 per cent. For this election Ben Gurion also brought to the fore a number of younger Mapai leaders who seem to share his views, including Abba Eban, the popular Ambassador to the United Nations, and General Moshe Dayan, the scholarly hero of the Sinai Campaign.

Ben Gurion has also been working to lessen the influence of political parties in the everyday life of Israel. He is trying to abolish the system of proportional representation which favors small parties, and to substitute for it a system of single seat districts such as that used in Great Britain or in the American House of Representatives.

Israel's political system was well developed even prior to its actual attainment of independence in 1948. Under the British mandate, the different Zionist political parties, of necessity, took the initiative in establishing agricultural settlements, schools, and industry. With the creation of the new state, however, the Israeli government took over much of this responsibility.

During the period of British rule, the so-called "party key system" was used in place of a civil service and also in order to divide authority. Under this system, each party would get a number of positions in the provisional government, and a proportion of Zionist funds approximately equivalent to the party's strength among the voters. Most of the jobs in the various national institutions were assigned on this basis. The system has been carried over into present-day Israel and has meant that most of the better jobs are obtainable on the basis of party membership rather than on merit. It has also meant that the parties have vested economic interests in different government departments and other Zionist or Histadrut institutions. Often elaborate and wasteful bureaucracies have developed. Although dishonesty among Israeli public officials is rare, the party key system has weakened their effectiveness and undermined their morale.

Although he recognizes the important services the various parties have performed in creating the state, Ben Gurion feels that the large number of economically powerful parties, each with its own narrow class or sectarian outlook, seriously impedes the progress of his nation. He has been particularly troubled by the necessity of giving extensive patronage and economic concessions to the different parties in order to maintain a coalition government. He wants a two-party system to develop in Israel similar to that of Great Britain.

Ben Gurion's opponents have very correctly pointed out that the middle-of-the-road Mapai would probably win a decisive majority of seats if his plans were adopted. Nevertheless, Ben Gurion's efforts to lessen the economic influence of Israel's political parties seems to be an important and far-sighted step toward strengthening his nation's political structure.

Israel today is a politically stable nation of over two million people with a standard of living as high as many countries of Europe. Although it has made unbelievable progress since 1948, it has a long way to go before it may be considered a fully Western nation comparable to Britain, France, or Belgium. Its factories are not nearly as efficient or productive as are similar factories in Western Europe, and the volume of its imports is about three times that of its exports. Loans and gifts from abroad, and German reparations, are responsible for the relatively high standard of living Israel enjoys.

The necessity for expending a high percentage of her resources on defense has been the main factor retarding Israel's economic development. Israel is surrounded almost entirely by hostile neighbors: the United Arab Republic of Egypt and Syria, Jordan, and Lebanon. The U.A.R. under Nasser is regarded as a particularly serious threat. Ben Gurion has followed a policy called "dynamic defense" which has involved keeping Israel partially mobilized, on the Swiss model, at all times. Although he has been a politician most of his life, Ben Gurion, in recent years, has been obliged to become an authority on military equipment and organization. Israel's powerful "Defense Army" is a monument to his work. It is as defense leader that the Israeli population is most unanimous in supporting Ben Gurion. The 1956 Sinai Operation, which set out to destroy the huge Egyptian bases on Israel's borders and to break the Egyptian blockade of Israel's southern port of Eilat, was in great part his handiwork.

The port of Eilat was especially important to Ben Gurion because he wished to expand Israel's commercial relations with Asia and with East Africa. Israel has had much success in establishing ties with a number of non-Arab Asian and African nations. It has great numbers of technicians, especially in agriculture and the sciences, and has sent many technical aid missions to underdeveloped states; Burma in Asia, and Ghana and Ethiopia in Africa have had especially close ties with Israel.

Although Israel's position as an independent and prosperous nation has been recognized by most non-Arab peoples, it will be the task of Israel, and of its leading statesman, Ben Gurion, to achieve amicable relations with the Arab nations. Cooperation between Israel and her neighbors is essential for the continuing prosperity of Israel and for the peace of the Near East. The achievement of harmonious relations will require all the genius and energy that Israel's leaders can command.

VIII BOURGUIBA OF TUNISIA: MODERATE
OF ARAB NATIONALISM

Habib Bouriguiba has said that "morally, independence always comes too slowly for the oppressed and too fast for the colonizers."

We have witnessed in our lifetimes the achievement of political independence by almost all of the European colonial possession in Asia and Africa. Yet resentment and envy of the great powers continues to smolder in the hearts of the newly emancipated peoples. Often, they are greatly tempted to brand as colonialistic every relationship with the advanced industrialized states. Often the outlook of the former colonial peoples is guided and molded, almost exclusively, by the personality and the wisdom of the man in power.

Nationalist movements in many of the underdeveloped countries of Asia, Africa, and Latin America take an extreme form: suspicion of foreigners, envy of the industrialized Western nations, intolerance of minorities, and an irrational hatred for the Western world. The great social problems and the sharp class divisions in these backward countries encourage fanaticism and a narrow outlook toward both foreign and domestic affairs. Perhaps the outstanding example of a moderate, far-sighted leader of an underdeveloped nation is Habib Bourguiba, President of Tunisia.

Although a lifelong nationalist and fighter against French colonialism, Bourguiba has consistently favored gradual and liberal policies and has supported the use of force only when all peaceful means of reaching an agreement have failed. Bourguiba is the founder and leader of perhaps the best organized nationalist movement in the non-Western world, the Neo-Destour, or New Constitution Party. The leaders of this party, including Bourguiba, are, culturally speaking, highly urbane Frenchmen; indeed many of them hardly know the native Arabic, or speak it with a marked

French accent. Yet, they are not levantine or cosmopolitans but are sincerely dedicated to the revitalization of the Tunisian nation, built upon a modernized Arabic-Islamic foundation. *Bourguibism*, the term used to denote the moderate and liberal policies which Bourguiba represents, is criticized and challenged in Arab North Africa, more especially by Egyptian President Nasser. Still, Bourguiba's ideas are very influential among leading North African Arabs, especially in the area known as the Mahgreb, made up of Morocco, Algeria and Tunisia. He is also the undisputed head and the greatest national hero of his homeland Tunisia.

Although his charismatic appeal is great, Bourguiba deliberately plays down the cult of the personality. He maintains a friendly and relaxed relationship with the common people and with his immediate subordinates, and goes out of his way to encourage informality. Bourguiba is unashamedly a lover of French culture and of the French liberal political tradition. He and the other leaders of the Neo-Destour are Moslems, but they seek to modernize their religion and rebuild Tunisia on the model of a Western nation, with no tie between church and state.

Tunisia, which is bordered by the sea on two sides, is a dry, semi-desert region. Along the coasts are wide plains, and the interior is largely mountainous. The topography of the country and the good natural harbors have directed Tunisians toward the sea and have brought sea-faring people to Tunisia since ancient times. Tunis, the capital of Tunisia, is near the site of the ancient city of Carthage. The country abounds in ruins; in fact some Roman aqueducts are still in use. Tunisia's strategic location in the heart of the Mediterranean world has made it a much sought-after prize of the great naval powers. It served as an important military base in World War II and the French today maintain a large naval installation at Bizerta, north of Tunis.

Tunisia is a nation of some four million people, predominantly Arabic-speaking Moslems. Most Tunisians are poverty-stricken farmers; and a small percentage of the population is still tribal. The country's only large city is Tunis, with a population of over 400,000. Tunisia has few natural resources and inadequate water for farming, although it has a great water power potential, and there are large underground lakes. The standard of living is very

Habib Bourguiba: *"Tunisia has chosen unequivocally to follow the free world of the West. But while rejecting Communism, it bears no enmity towards the nations which live under a communist regime. Every one of them should have the right to live under the ideological and economic system which suits it best. . . ."*

low, the average income being about *one hundred dollars per year.*
Although significant progress has been made, disease and illiteracy
are still widespread.

From the 16th to the 19th century, Tunisia was ruled by a *bey,*
actually independent, but nominally an official of the Ottoman
Turkish Empire. In the 19th century France extended her influence and authority to the three Mahgreb states, Morocco,
Tunisia, and Algeria. The largest and richest of the three, Algeria, was incorporated by the French as an integral part of France.
In theory, as French Algerian settlers put it today, Algiers is as
much a part of France as is Paris. In contrast, Morocco and Tunisia
were allowed to keep their nominal independence under their local
rulers, and to become "protectorates"—actually colonies of France.
By 1883 France had consolidated her control of Tunisia. With
French political control there came a great influx of French schools
and other French cultural influences. A growing number of
Arabs in the Mahgreb became Westernized, largely in the French
tradition. Also, large numbers of French and other European
Christian settlers, the so-called Colons, migrated to the Mahgreb
countries, often establishing large and prosperous agricultural estates and employing native Arabs as workers. Nationalist sentiment began to show itself very early as a reaction to French control, especially among the Western-educated Arabs.

In 1908, a Westernized nationalist group, called the Young
Turks, seized power in Ottoman Turkey and inspired Tunisian
Arab nationalists to set up a similar body called the Young Tunisians. This group favored the establishment of a liberal constitutional regime and the elimination of foreign political influence
from their homeland.

World War I was the major turning point for Tunisian nationalism. By this time a Westernized Arab middle class had developed,
greatly influenced by Woodrow Wilson's ideas on national self-
determination as expressed in his widely publicized Fourteen Points.
During the war the French had also provoked the more reactionary
Islamic elments in Tunisia by threatening to confiscate lands of
the Islamic institutions. As a result, a united Tunisian delegation,
representing the Westernized Young Tunisians and the traditionalist Islamic leaders, presented a petition to the Paris Peace

Conference in 1919, demanding independence for Tunisia.

Although frustrated by the French at the peace conference, these two elements the following year formed the Destour, or Constitution Party. The Destour Party sought an independent constitutional government under the bey, built on liberal principles, including civil rights and universal suffrage. During the 1920's, the Destour Party grew in strength and organization, but was never capable of seriously challenging the French rule.

In 1933 the younger and more militant nationalists within the Destour Party under the leadership of a young lawyer, Habib Bourguiba, broke away and founded Tunisia's present governing party, the Neo-Destour.

Bourguiba was born in 1903 into a middle class family deeply involved in nationalist activity. As a student in a French high school in Tunis, he joined the Destour Party. At the age of 19, he went to Paris for five years to study law. There he led meetings and discussions with other young Tunisian nationalists. Like many other Westernized Tunisians studying in France, he married a French girl. From the time of his return to Tunisia he was continually involved in nationalist activities, much of the period being spent either in a French jail or in exile. By 1934 he was established as the leading militant nationalist, and he became the secretary general, or effective head, of the Neo-Destour.

Under his guidance the Neo-Destour mobilized most of the Tunisian nationalists into its ranks. Bourguiba built it on a hierarchical, totalitarian model, with local units, or cells, in every village and with the chain of command rising to him. Other components of the party, such as trade unions, youth brigades, and women's groups, permitted it to permeate most of Tunisian society.

During World War II nationalist strength in Tunisia grew, and after the war the French were forced to make increased concessions to the Neo-Destour. Finally, after protracted negotiations and some bloodshed, in March, 1956, the French government and the Neo-Destour leadership concluded an agreement recognizing the independence of Tunisia. At this time Bourguiba made his triumphal return to Tunisia to assume the direct leadership of the country.

The most dramatic thing about Bourguiba's leadership has been his effort to break the ties of the past and make Tunisia a modern,

Westernized state. In 1957, he ended the traditional institution of the bey, and made Tunisia a republic. In July, he was elected first president of this Tunisian Republic. Under his guidance a new constitution was approved in June, 1959, which made Tunisia largely a secular state. The constitution took away from religious officials much of their arbitrary authority in matters of personal status, such as marriage, divorce and inheritance; and it basically removed historic political powers which church groups had enjoyed in Moslem countries.

Bourguiba has campaigned vigorously to persuade Tunisian Moslems to emancipate themselves from outmoded customs and to bring their religious habits up to date. The month-long fast of Ramadan, during which Moslems abstain from all food and drink in the daylight hours received his criticism as being out of step with 20th-century living and harmful to the progress of the nation. He urged Tunisians to adopt European-style clothing and the European way of life. He is especially concerned with the status of Moslem women, and in the liberal tradition wishes to emancipate them socially as well as politically. Frequently in public, he will playfully try to remove veils from women he meets, and he has given much support to women's groups seeking to end their traditional abject subservience to their husbands and fathers.

Since its creation the Neo-Destour has been in the vanguard of efforts to modernize Tunisia. It serves as the nucleus in the attempted transformation of Tunisia from a theocratic, Oriental state to a modernized European nation. The party cells of the villages and cities, and other supporting groups continually agitate against the traditional way of life. Because the Neo-Destour has many thousands of Western-educated and disciplined members who share Bourguiba's determination to reconstruct their national life, Tunisia is the most advanced of the Moslem Arab nations in North Africa or the Middle East in adjusting to the demands of a Western, nationalist society. The contrast between East and West, however, is still strikingly evident.

Bourguiba's success or failure in Tunisia will probably depend on his ability to improve the critical economic conditions there. With few natural resources, no industry, and little capital, the powerful political structure he has built could easily fall apart if the low standard of living is not raised.   Unemployment today is estimated at 25 per cent, and there is a great need for improving the efficiency of those who are employed.   Much of Tunisia's skilled labor and most of her industry and capital were French. The departure of many of the French colons after 1955 and the partial closing of the French market to the high-cost Tunisian agricultural products, have left a serious gap in the Tunisian economy.   Because of his great affection for the French way of life and because Tunisia is not economically viable, Bourguiba has advocated maintaining close ties with France.   The 1956 treaty which gave Tunisia its independence was deliberately vague as to the exact relationship, political and economic, between the two countries.   The French have continued to give Tunisia economic and technical aid, but in decreasing amounts.   Bourguiba, and the French as well, would probably like a relationship between the two countries similar to that of the British Commonwealth or of the new French Community.   The war in Algeria, however, has prevented any such tie from developing.

Tunisia is an Arab nation, and linguistically and religiously, is at one with the Arab rebels in Algeria.   Bourguiba has repeatedly said that as far as this war is concerned, Tunisia is not neutral, and he continually refers to the Arab rebels as "my brothers."   To the great annoyance of the French he has allowed Tunisia to be used as a supply base and headquarters for the National Liberation Front, the organization leading the revolt.   The French, in a vain effort to stop rebels from using Tunisian bases, have built elaborate barbed-wire fortifications along the lengthy Algeria-Tunisian border.   They have also pursued rebel units into Tunisia; and on one occasion in 1958 on a reprisal action, they bombed a Tunisian border village, believed to be a rebel base.   As a result, a number of Tunisian women and children were killed; nationalist opinion in Tunisia was brought to a high pitch; and Bourguiba's relations with France were greatly strained.

Bourguiba, nevertheless, has advised the Algerian rebels to be moderate and to work to find a basis for a peaceful settlement with the French.   Although he does not always condemn the use of terrorist methods, he urges patience and logic in the struggle for independence.   It is widely believed that Bourguiba's restraining influence has prevented the Algerian rebels from seeking the all-out aid of the Soviet Union and has minimized the importance of the Communists' role in Algeria and Tunisia.

The leaders of the Algerian rebellion, like Bourguiba, have close cultural ties with France—many of them speak French and often do not know Arabic. An ideal solution to end the long and bloody Algerian War might be the formation of a confederation of the three Mahgreb states—Morocco, Tunisia, and Algeria—a confederation which could then be joined to France and Europe through a voluntary association of states such as the Common Market. De Gaulle and other moderate French leaders have been working in this direction but are being opposed by ultra-nationalist sentiment in France and among the French settlers in Algeria. Bourguiba's moderate policies, are correspondingly resisted by extreme Arab nationalists, who wish to break all connections with the European colonial powers. Yet, such a Mahgreb Confederation, joined perhaps to the existing Common Market, could meet the legitimate desires of all sides in the controversy. The North African Arabs would receive their long-sought-after independence and national unity; French national pride would be served by the cultural and economic ties between France and over 20 million Moslems in North Africa. The one million French settlers in Algeria would not be isolated, as they so frantically fear, from France and Europe, and their special economic position in Algeria would be at least partially protected by the absence of economic frontiers between Common Market nations.

Until the Algerian War is ended, there can be no peace or stability for Tunisia. Bourguiba, to keep himself in power, must appease Tunisian nationalist sentiment by opposing French policies in Algeria; and, as long as he opposes France, the French will not give Tunisia the large-scale economic aid that she so desperately needs. Moreover, France has been able to persuade her Western allies, including the United States, to limit their aid to Tunisia.

Gamel Nasser of Egypt, has represented the extremist school of Arab nationalism, and has been the arch-enemy of Bourguiba. Nasser, while denouncing Bourguiba's policies as a betrayal of Arab interests to the Western colonial powers, has often allied himself with the Soviet Union and has accepted extensive Soviet military aid. Cairo has become the center for violent denunciations of the West; the French have long recognized that Egypt is the main headquarters and supply depot for the extremist elements among the Algerian rebels. Nasser has actively campaigned to overthrow Bourguiba. He has sheltered and supported Salah Ben Yusuf, a former leader of the Neo-Destour, and now Bourguiba's principle Tunisian political rival. With Nasser's aid, ultra-nationalist supporters of Ben Yusuf tried to overthrow Bourguiba in 1956. At least one assassination attempt on Tunisia's president by followers of Ben Yusuf has been made. Curiously, Nasser has encouraged both right-wing and left-wing opposition to Bourguiba: the traditionalist elements in Tunisian society, who are fearful of Bourguiba's secular and equalitarian views and the far left wing, made up of Communists and doctrinaire Socialists, who are hostile to the West, and suspicious of Bourguiba's liberal economic policies.

While extremists, such as Nasser, seek to attack and undermine Bourguiba's government, those committed to the cause of democratic principles find in him an important spokesman. And in the long run it will be through the path of moderation and non-violence —such as Bourguiba is following—that Arab Africa will best attain its democratic goals.

Jawaharlal Nehru: *"I have become a queer mixture of east and west, out of place everywhere, and at home nowhere. . . . Mother India is to me a beautiful lady, very old, but very youthful in appearance, sad eyed and forlorn, cruelly treated by aliens and outsiders, and calling upon her children to protect her. . . . And yet India is in the main the peasant and the worker, not beautiful to look at, for poverty is not beautiful."*

IX NEHRU OF INDIA: SPOKESMAN FOR NEUTRALIST ASIA

We of the Western world are today trying to win over the uncommitted peoples of Asia and Africa to the democratic way of life. The democratic faith is based on the idea that the citizen will have the ability and the desire to comprehend the great issues of the day. Sadly though, even in our supposedly advanced and literate society, the voter is often influenced by a multitude of irrational and irrelevant considerations in the choice of his leaders. But the problem of communicating the democratic credo in countries that are predominantly illiterate is a staggering one.

The successful leader in the underdeveloped nation must, therefore, try to understand the unarticulated aspirations, or, as it were, the subconscious mind of his people. The ability to dramatize and simplify the issues, to present his program in understandable symbols—these often mark the success of the man in power.

Two-thirds of the world's population live in the underdeveloped nations of Asia, Africa, and Latin America. Among these people, there is an increasing demand for better living conditions and for some of the luxuries of life; this demand has been described as "the revolution of rising expectancies."

Modern communications, especially radio and films, are rapidly breaking down the walls of isolation around these people, and are making them aware of the higher standards of living enjoyed by the more industrialized countries.

Sadly, however, many of the underdeveloped nations must face a basic dilemma: despite industrialization, their skyrocketing populations make it difficult to maintain even the present low living standards; yet their newly-awakening citizens are impatiently demanding spectacular improvements.

Two major and competing political forms, *liberalism* and *totalitarianism,* are being offered as answers to this dilemma.

The *liberal* solution is based on a government and society which recognizes individual freedom and initiative as the means to carry out the education and industrialization necessary for a higher standard of living. Persuasion rather than force is the liberal method of achieving desirable national goals.

The *totalitarian* solution, on the other hand, would subordinate individual rights and would have the nation mobilized into an army of workers. All aspects of life—religious, cultural, domestic and political—would be controlled and directed for the advancement of the state. Red China is the best recent example of an underdeveloped nation adopting this totalitarian method.

The appeal of communism to the underdeveloped peoples is not based on abstract theory but on practical example. The apparent successes of the totalitarian-Communist regimes in China and the Soviet Union have caused many to believe that totalitarianism is the better solution.

The best recent example of an underdeveloped nation to adopt the liberal solution is India. Although not a democracy as we understand it, India's government is based on liberal parliamentary institutions and allows much individual freedom and responsibility.

Prime Minister Nehru of India is perhaps the outstanding example of a major leader who has directed his underdeveloped nation along the liberal road. No other contemporary figure can equal Nehru's charismatic appeal or claim the reverence of so many devoted followers. Nehru sincerely believes in government by the consent of the governed and has scrupulously adhered to a parliamentary, democratic framework for India; nevertheless, he completely controls his government. His great authority stems from two sources: his unrivalled appeal to the masses and his influence and control over the National Congress Party. His ideal is democracy; but he knows that for his backward and divided people, democracy must for the present, remain a goal.

Nehru is the heir and disciple of India's greatest modern leader, Mahatma Gandhi. In contrast to Gandhi, who believed that direct, though non-violent, action was the best means of achieving results, Nehru advocates mediation and compromise in solving problems.

Nehru has consistently sought to tone down the many religious and regional divisions among Indians and to forge India into a unified nation. In international affairs he has been a leader in the struggle to lessen Cold War tensions. His advocacy of co-existence between the United States and the Soviet Union corresponds to his view of bringing harmony into his own divided nation.

Although Nehru often gives the impression of being a utopian in his social philosophy, the record clearly indicates that he is a practical politician. He has often been indecisive in his leadership, but he does have one overriding political objective: to unite India and to make it a modern and prosperous nation. He wants India to secularize itself, to throw off the shackles of custom and habit and to adopt Western technology. Like Gandhi, Nehru is primarily a teacher and his greatest contribution has been in inspiring young Indians to dedicate themselves to the modernization of their country.

India has been described as not so much a nation, as a congregation of nations. It has within it many different nationalities, each speaking a distinct language. The government is in the form of a federal republic with fourteen member states. Hindi, an Indo-European tongue, is the official language, but more that half the population is unfamiliar with this language. With the separation from India in 1947 of Moslem Pakistan, 90 per cent of the Indian people are of the Hindu faith. Hinduism is the main unifying element of the country's varied population, and the rich and ancient Hindu accomplishments in philosophy, literature and art are something that all Indians can look upon with pride. Most of India's nationalities, however, have also had long and distinctive histories, often involving wars with other Indian nationalities. The feeling of separatism is deeply rooted, and the common Hindu tradition only partially binds together India's diverse nationalities.

It has been said that there is a "conscious" and a "subconscious" India. Conscious India, 5 per cent of the population, is made up of people educated and trained in the Western tradition. This 5 per cent, living largely in the great cities, often dresses in Western-style clothing and lives in the fashion of Americans or Europeans. Their ways of thinking and their general goals in life are similar to ours. This type of Indian goes abroad as a student or visitor and has been the backbone of the Congress Party. This group provides the nucleus for India's Westernized leadership upon whom Nehru depends.

"Subconscious India" is the 95 per cent that lives in a world of fantasy, superstition, witchcraft and religious taboos. It is composed of the great mass of illiterate peasants, the *fakirs,* or holy men, and the tens of millions of untouchables. The heart and soul of this subconscious India is the caste system which is deeply ingrained in the Hindu tradition. Hinduism puts great emphasis on what a man is and does — on birth and social conduct, rather than on a particular creed or theological belief. It is much more "otherworldly" in practice than are our Western religions.

The caste system is built, traditionally, around a feudalistic order of society, based on four descending groups. The Brahmin or priestly aristocratic caste is on top; the warrior caste is next, followed by the merchant and agricultural caste. The lowest cast is made up of the common laborers and artisans. In subconscious India there is no intermingling of the castes and there is widespread segregation and discrimination by the upper castes against the lower. The caste system apparently originated as a form of segregation based on color, the lighter skinned Indians wishing to place themselves above those of darker skin; the Hindi word for caste, "varna," is translated "color." Several centuries of British rule and the leadership of Nehru and the Congress Party have not yet influenced this 95 per cent of the Indian population.

By the 18th century, the British had made themselves masters of India, bringing order, and ending several centuries of political chaos. Remaining in power until 1947, they made many economic and political contributions which endure to this day. They built railroads, schools, and trained a native civil service, but they did not attempt to interfere with the caste system.

Under the British, great numbers of Indians were introduced to Western ways and many thousands studied in Britain. English became the *lingua franca* of India's educated class, and remains so today despite efforts to make Hindi a truly national tongue.

Nationalist feeling developed against the British, however, and in 1885 Westernized Indians, desiring independence for their homeland, established the Congress Party which welded together people of greatly diversified economic, political and religious views. The prestige and influence which it commanded among the masses as the principal spokesman for independence has enabled the Congress Party today to remain in power. Although it has not developed the rigid hierarchy typical of totalitarian parties, it is highly organized, having local and regional chapters throughout India, and it now claims a membership of 30 million.

The man most responsible for driving the British from India was Mahatma Gandhi. Although a Western-educated lawyer, he turned his back on Western ways and became a mystic in the Hindu tradition. He sought to reform individual morality and political practices as well. Traveling about India in his loincloth, Gandhi came to be regarded as a saint by the Hindu masses. By 1920, he was the best known critic of British rule and was the effective leader of the Congress party.

Gandhi had a profound understanding of the Indian mind and used symbolic actions to dramatize his teachings. Although he sought to end many of India's ancient social abuses, especially the caste system which condemned millions to low and degrading occupations, he opposed the modernization and industrialization of India as a threat to its traditional customs. He wished to preserve the village as the focal point of Indian life. He symbolized his opposition to modern technology and to the importation of British manufactured textiles by advocating home spinning, and in his journeys through villages, he would regularly stop and spin to demonstrate his belief.

Gandhi was a humanitarian and dedicated his life to ending bitterness and strife based on religious and national prejudices. His urging of equal treatment for India's Moslem minority shocked many devout Hindus and in 1948, on his way to a prayer meeting, he was assassinated by a Hindu fanatic. The mantle of Gandhi's leadership fell to his outstanding disciple, Nehru.

Nehru was born in 1889 of an aristocratic Brahmin family. His father, a highly successful lawyer, was a great admirer of the English and their culture, and young Nehru grew up with English as his mother tongue. At the age of 15, he was sent to England where he attended Harrow and then studied at Cambridge. He returned to India eight years later thoroughly Anglicized, apparently ready to settle down to a fashionable and comfortable life.

Nationalist feeling in India was growing stronger at this time, and young Nehru soon identified himself with the Congress Party and the freedom movement. While in Britain he was influenced by the Fabian Socialists, especially George Bernard Shaw, and he entered the Congress Party with a mildly socialistic and agnostic outlook. He took part in nationalist meetings and began to travel around India, for the first time becoming familiar with the condition of the Indian masses.

He soon became a disciple of Gandhi and by the early 1930's, Gandhi acknowledged him as his political heir. Although he had great respect for Gandhi's saintly qualities and for his success in mobilizing India against the British, he nevertheless found many of the older man's ideas and actions repugnant. Nehru was a frequent critic of Gandhi's mystical approach and especially his resistance to technological advancements.

During the period 1930-47 Nehru was in the forefront of the struggle against the British and because of his views, he, with thousands of other Congress Party members, spent much of this period in jail.

In 1947, Britain granted India independence and Nehru became the first prime minister of free India. Gandhi once described Nehru as being "more English than Indian in his thought and makeup." Certainly, the influence of Western secular and scientific methods is reflected in his outlook.

Nehru as prime minister has been sensitive to the religious traditions of the masses, and although he opposed Gandhi's emphasis on mysticism and glorification of village life, Nehru himself often evokes his predecessor's memory. He annually performs the spinning ritual in public, lives austerely, and now, in the Hindu tradition, refrains from eating meat. Like Gandhi, Nehru continues to travel throughout India, lecturing and cajoling the people to be more tolerant and to reject the caste system. He further urges that they emancipate themselves from superstitious practices, and that they stop venerating him like a god. Frequently, when he speaks, crowds who do not understand his words will come to see him and, if possible, touch his clothing.

Under Nehru, India has made spectacular economic and political advances. Large industries have been developed, and health and educational facilities have been built. Two successful five-year plans have been carried out, causing a great expansion in India's economic and industrial production. In 1952, Nehru's government inaugurated a systematic program designed to aid India's large rural population and to improve village life. Blocks of 100 villages were organized as development units, and a staff of experts were assigned to each unit to introduce new methods of sanitation and agriculture. Many millions of farmers have been aided and influenced by this program.

India still faces gigantic problems which could undo all of Nehru's work unless they are overcome. There is still a desperate shortage of food, and unemployment is widespread. India's skyrocketing population is at the root of her major problems. Even India's higher productivity rate, and the benefits of recent agricultural and industrial advances, have failed to keep step with her rapid growth in population.

There is also a serious question as to whether or not the Congress Party can hold together without Nehru. Now that the goal of independence has been attained, sharp intra-party factions have emerged, reflecting India's religious and regional differences. Alleged corruption among certain Congress Party leaders has turned many younger Indians to the small but highly-organized Communist Party. Nehru himself, although declaring that the Congress Party is the framework for India's progress, has been among its sharpest critics. In 1959 he stated that "provincialism, casteism and religious rivalries have developed within the party to a shameful degree."

In spite of these difficulties, Nehru is now launching a third five-year plan and is imposing heavy taxes on the Indian population to carry it out. The United States will undoubtedly make a major contribution in support of it. Since 1956, we have given India over 3 billion dollars in aid and it is probable that this amount will be doubled during the present five-year plan.

Many Americans have had serious doubts about Nehru. They are annoyed by his socialistic language and are suspicious of his neutralist policy of non-alignment in the Cold War. They cannot understand why a leader who favors democracy should frequently defend and even support policies of the Soviet Union and Red China.   Nehru's attitude is partly based on an innocent optimism which he shares with other neutralist leaders, but it is also founded on the recognition that any involvement in war would destroy India's economic and political achievements.   As a realist, he also knows that India cannot afford to antagonize her two powerful Communist neighbors.   Nehru has said that communism is simply another aggressive, evangelical faith, which like many other crusading creeds, will in time moderate itself and find a peaceful basis for coexistence.

Throughout his career, Nehru has criticized Communist methods, and has frequently suppressed Communist activity in India and arrested large numbers of suspected Communists.   Even at the height of the 1959 Red Chinese incursions into India's border provinces, however, Nehru tried to isolate this dispute from the general Cold War conflict.   He has long believed that disputes such as this cannot be solved if they become enmeshed in the East-West struggle.

By his own people, Nehru may well be remembered as the man who held India together, and gave it over a decade of national unity and peaceful progress.   In a larger sense, he will be regarded by the uncommitted millions of Africa and Asia as the man who—perhaps more than any other powerful world figure—worked tirelessly in the interests of world peace through the "middle path" of neutralism.

X EAMON DE VALERA: FIGHTER FOR IRISH INDEPENDENCE

Eamon de Valera, President and foremost figure of independent Ireland, has directed his nation's destiny for almost four decades. De Valera, an American by birth, was a professsor of mathematics by profession. Early in life, he was inspired by Irish nationalism and served as a revolutionist and underground fighter for his adopted homeland. Although a leader in the bloody 1916 revolt against Great Britain and in the even more savage Irish Civil War of the early 1920's, De Valera has always been a moderate in politics and has hated violence and bloodshed.

He has dedicated his life to making Ireland a free and equal member of the family of nations, and has sought to revive an awareness and a pride of the historic language and civilization of his people. One of his most ardent desires has been to end the centuries-old hatred between the Irish and English nationalities and to heal the wounds of religious strife which have separated these two peoples for so long.

Historically, the Irish, with the Scots and the Welsh, are descendants of the ancient Celts who ruled the British Isles 2000 years ago. A form of Celtic, Gaelic, is still spoken by about 10 per cent of the Irish people. Although England was conquered and ruled by the Roman Empire, the fiercely independent Irish and Scots were not, and they retained much of their old Celtic language, customs and political institutions. Even the introduction of Christianity into Ireland in the fifth century apparently did not greatly change the character of Irish life. The Catholic Church in Ireland to this day has had a distinctive personality and outlook.

By the 14th century, the English had become the most numerous and best organized nationality in the British Isles, and they proceeded to conquer the three neighboring peoples—the Welsh, the Irish, and the Scots. The Welsh and Scots still differentiate themselves from the English, but are content to accept the leadership of London, sharing with the English a common British nationality. For religious reasons, however, the Irish did not merge with the English as did the other two Celtic peoples.

In the Protestant Reformation of the 16th and 17th centuries, Ireland remained Roman Catholic while the other British peoples became Protestant. This religious difference has been at the root of Irish resistance to English domination. Oliver Cromwell, the 17th-century Puritan ruler of England, was especially severe in supressing rebellion in Ireland, and he greatly inflamed religious hatred between the two peoples. At this time, large numbers of Protestants from Scotland and England were settled in Ireland. Today, the descendants of these settlers make up a Protestant minority of about 25 per cent of the Irish population. Most of these live in Ulster, the six northern counties, where they constitute a majority.

The Republic of Ireland is today the smallest of the island nations of the world, having an area about twice the size of Massachusetts. Its population is approximately 3 million; another 1.4 million Irishmen live in Ulster.

Ireland has been and remains basically an agricultural country, but the climate and rocky soil are not well suited for efficient farming. Much of the interior land is used for the raising of pedigreed horses and of beef cattle, Ireland being a major exporter of meat products. In recent years there has been a sizable exodus from the farm to the city, and a growing number of Irishmen now work in industry and white-collar professions; a small majority, however, are still employed in agriculture. Because Ireland was governed for so long by the English, class differences among Irishmen did not develop, and socially speaking, it is one of the most homogeneous nations in the world. Also, because the church was not connected with the ruling group, Ireland does not have a legacy of anticlericalism which divides and weakens other Catholic countries of Europe such as France, Italy, and Spain.

Dublin, with a population of 600,000, is Ireland's only major city and is the cultural and political heart of the nation. It was

Eamon de Valera: *"Ireland must mean not the purple hills and the green fields merely, but . . . the men and women of the Nation—the souls that can agonize and suffer."*

the scene of much of the resistance to the English in the early part of this century, and its streets and parks are filled with monuments to the outstanding political and literary figures of the land.

The great famine of 1847 was the turning point in modern Irish history. Over 700,000 died of hunger and an equal number emigrated, largely to the United States. From 1847 to 1951 Ireland's population steadily declined, dropping from 8 million to about 4 million. Most of this decrease was due to a continuous emigration of many of the more vigorous and ambitious people of the country. Ireland was too weakened by the famine and emigration to join with other oppressed nationalities and throw out foreign rule in the nationalist revolutions which swept Europe in 1848. The 20th century found the Irish one of the few major nationalities in Western Europe that felt itself dominated and oppressed by another power.

Irish nationalism did develop, however, and the question of self-government for Ireland was continually before the British Parliament in the late 19th and early 20th centuries. Prior to World War I most Irish nationalists were moderate in their demands and did not seek to break completely with London. But as early as 1858, a more extreme organization, called the Irish Republican Brotherhood, was formed, and it wanted no ties of any sort with Great Britain.

The efforts to gain home rule for Ireland were frustrated in great part by Ireland's Protestant minority. Although there were many Protestants in the Irish nationalist movement, most were fearful of being ruled by the Catholic majority, and they were able to get enough support in England to defeat home-rule proposals. By 1914, many Irish nationalists had despaired of achieving independence by peaceful, parliamentary means, and the outbreak of war seemed to offer an opportunity for action.

At this time, the important nationalist organization was the *Sinn Fein*—Gaelic for "Ourselves Alone." The Sinn Fein leadership concluded that extreme steps had to be taken to expel the British. Irish nationalists had long said that "England's difficulty is Ireland's opportunity." Irishmen were now urged to serve the interests of their own country rather than those of England. Irish volunteer units were formed which pledged to serve "neither King nor Kaiser," but to fight for Irish freedom. Sinn Fein leaders did, however, approach the Germans for aid, and this greatly provoked the British Government. In Easter week of 1916, a revolt led by the Sinn Fein broke out in Dublin and in other parts of Ireland, but it was soon suppressed by the British Government, and most of its leaders arrested and executed.

One of the captured leaders of the Easter Rebellion, Eamon de Valera, primarily because of the accident of his birth, had his death sentence commuted to life imprisonment. De Valera was born in New York City in 1882 to an immigrant Irish mother and a Spanish father. When he was two, his father died, and he was sent to live with relatives in Ireland. At an early age he showed the qualities of perseverance and thoroughness which have marked him throughout his life. He won several scholarships to secondary school and the university, and by the age of 22 was established as a competent teacher and a promising mathematician. He joined the Sinn Fein but remained somewhat opposed to the extremism shown by the Irish Republican Brotherhood. As a Sinn Fein member he had also joined the Irish Volunteers, the main military body of the Irish nationalists, and by 1916 he was a battalion commander. Although De Valera believed that Irishmen should not fight for Britain as long as they were subjugated, he also opposed the decision to rebel, but he was overruled by the more militant leaders in the Sinn Fein, and, as a good soldier, he accepted orders.

De Valera was released from prison in a general amnesty granted in 1917 and soon became the leading Irish spokesman for resistance to the British. In the next few years Ireland was in a state of constant revolt, with nationalists waging incessant guerrilla warfare against the British. Through this period De Valera was in and out of jail several times.

Finally, in July 1921, the British Prime Minister, Lloyd George, and De Valera concluded a truce agreement. The following December, over the opposition of De Valera, other Irish nationalist leaders concluded the Anglo-Irish Treaty with the British. This treaty provided that Ireland would become a British dominion similar to Canada or Australia and would be free to conduct her own affairs. This part was quite agreeable to De Valera. But the treaty also provided that the six northern counties with their Protestant majority would not be part of the new Irish Free State. This provision De Valera and many other nationalists refused to accept.

The nationalist leaders who accepted the treaty believed, with much logic, that it was a forward step toward full independence, and they felt Ireland desperately needed peace. The opponents of the treaty, Republicans led by De Valera, believed that it was a betrayal. A great split developed among Irish nationalists. A majority of the Sinn Fein members supported De Valera, but a sizable minority gave their support to the new Irish Free State government, led by William Cosgrave, who served as prime minister from 1922 to 1932. In the beginning, at least, a great part of the Irish population also supported Cosgrave's government.

De Valera opposed the treaty agreement and advocated a non-violent boycott of the new government. However, many disregarded his advice and resorted to force. The Irish Republican Army was formed to combat the treaty and the Free State government. Soon Irishmen were fighting Irishmen, wreaking bloodshed and destruction throughout the country. By 1923, over 11,000 Republicans, including De Valera, were in jail.

De Valera was horrified by the civil war and reluctantly decided to end his boycott of the Free State government. In 1926, he led a large group of his supporters out of the Sinn Fein and formed his own party, the *Fianna Fail*—"Warriors of Fate." Having won a seat in the Free State Parliament, De Valera swallowed his pride and took the oath of allegiance to the British King, with a large group of Fianna Fail members, so that they could legally take their seats in the Parliament. From 1926 to 1932 De Valera was leader of the opposition to the Cosgrave government. The Fianna Fail committed itself to end all ties with Britain, to unite with Northern Ireland and to initiate a program of economic self-sufficiency. In 1932 De Valera was able to form a coalition government and became prime minister of the Irish Free State.

Except for two three-year periods, 1948-1951 and 1954-1957 De Valera served as prime minister until 1959. In that year, he voluntarily resigned and became the non-political president of the republic. One of his key lieutenants, Sean Lemass, succeeded him, and is the prime minister at the present time.

One of De Valera's main concerns in his early years as prime minister was the question of relations with Britain. He worked continuously to complete the break which the 1921 Treaty had begun. One of his first moves was to refuse to hand over to the British revenues collected before the establishment of the Free State. London soon retaliated with taxes on Irish imports and for several years a full-scale customs war was waged between the two countries. It was at this time that De Valera inaugurated a policy of making Ireland economically self-sufficient. His government subsidized and protected local industry, and especially encouraged the development of Ireland's rich peat and water power resources.

In 1931, the British government enacted the famous Statute of Westminster, which allowed all of the dominions the full right of self-government. Under this authority De Valera changed Ireland into a republic in 1937, but, technically at least, the country remained a British dominion.

When World War II broke out, Ireland was the only dominion to remain neutral. De Valera recognized that anti-British feeling was so strong among many Irish nationalists that any hint of Irish government support of the English would throw the country again into civil war. He did promise Britain, though, that Ireland would not allow its territory to be used as a base for attacking Britain.

In 1949 the last links connecting Ireland with Britain were broken when the Irish government declared itself an independent republic. The British government, perhaps repentant, accepted this, and agreed further to allow Ireland the economic privileges that go with dominion membership. Irishmen may come and go in the United Kingdom without restrictions. In recent years, almost all emigrants from Ireland have settled in England, and most of Ireland's trade is still with Britain. De Valera has favored this turn of events and has maintained close contacts with the leaders of the British government.

The great unresolved problem that disturbs Anglo-Irish relations is the question of the status of the six northern counties. De Valera has said that no Irishman will be satisfied until the whole of Ireland is united. Partition is a constant reminder of past conflicts and hatreds. For more than 30 years, over the opposition of De Valera and of most other Irish leaders, the underground Irish Republican Army has tried to end partition by violence, shootings, and the dynamiting of police stations and other public buildings in Ulster. In 1936, De Valera declared the Irish Republican Army to be an illegal organization and had some success in suppressing it. Although the I.R.A. today is numerically insignificant, much of its membership consisting of adventuresome teenagers, it still commands much sympathy and support among the general Irish public.

De Valera in recent years has suggested the establishment of a federal relationship between the North and the South which would allow the six counties to have a large degree of self-government. This in the long run would seem to be the best solution. At the present time, however, this issue seems to be clouded with so much suspicion and intolerance that it would be difficult to end partition by any peaceful means.

Since World War II, De Valera has favored a policy of economic liberalism in order to help raise Ireland's standard of living through industrialization. The Irish government has conducted a systematic campaign to encourage foreign businessmen and industry to invest in Ireland. Industrial exhibits and trade fairs are regularly held to demonstrate Ireland's economic advantages. The latest British and American tractors and farm machinery, assembled in Ireland, are shown alongside the pedigreed cattle for which the country is famous. These exhibitions are held as much for the tourist as for the foreign businessman. The tourist industry is second only to agriculture as a source of the nation's revenue.

The Irish government's liberal economic policy has been demonstrated not only by exhibitions and fairs but by a very favorable tax policy toward the profits of foreign investments. As a result, scores of American, German and French business firms have established manufacturing and processing plants throughout Ireland.

De Valera has also been a leader in the movement to revive Gaelic and make it the national tongue in place of English. As a young man, he came under the influence of Douglas Hyde, the poet and philosopher who was to become Ireland's first president in 1937. Hyde had founded the Gaelic League in 1893, and this organization became the main force seeking to make Gaelic a modern and dynamic language. Since 1922, the Irish government has encouraged and sponsored the use of Gaelic. A thorough knowledge of it is mandatory for most public school teachers, and courses in the language are given in the schools and universities. In spite of all these attempts, however, English continues to be the common language and none of the important Irish writers use Gaelic. Although there is no formal opposition to the teaching and use of Gaelic, some Irish leaders are fearful that a very strong emphasis on it will cause students to become illiterate in two languages rather than proficient in one.

A problem which has greatly concerned De Valera has been Ireland's declining population. This decline has been caused by the high rate of emigration and also by a low marriage rate. Although the great famine of 1847 was the dramatic turning point of emigration from Ireland, for centuries before this time, Irish emigrants, especially professional soldiers, were found all over the world.

In the 19th and early 20th centuries, tens of thousands left Ireland annually, mainly for the new world. There are an estimated 30 million people of Irish extraction in the United States alone. One of the reasons for De Valera's initial prestige among Irish nationalists was his American birth, and the belief that he symbolized the interest and sympathy of many Americans in the struggle for Irish independence. De Valera has frequently invited young men and women of Irish ancestry from abroad to settle in Ireland and contribute their technical skills to the rebuilding of the nation.

Although De Valera no longer plays an active role in Irish politics, he has left an indelible imprint upon his government and upon the thinking of his countrymen.

Abubakar Tafawa Balewa: *"We consider it wrong for the Federal Government [of Nigeria] to associate itself as a matter of routine with any of the power blocs. . . . Our policies will be founded on Nigeria's interests and will be consistent with the moral and democratic principles on which our constitution is based."*

XI ABUBAKAR OF NIGERIA: SYMBOL OF RISING AFRICA

One outstanding characteristic seems to mark the successful man of power—his seemingly immeasurable ability to persuade and inspire his people to compromise and moderate their desires for the common good. The enlightened leader, especially in the less developed nations, must wage a continual struggle against fanaticism and parochialism.

Nowhere are the demands greater on the leader, and nowhere is the influence of his personality and judgment more significant that among the newly-born nations of Africa. Over half of Africa's 200 million people have now received their independence and in all likelihood the remaining half will soon achieve or be given national freedom.

Africa may be divided racially into two main parts: the area north of the Sahara Desert, bordering the Mediterranean, which is inhabited largely by light-skinned, Arabic-speaking peoples, numbering some 40 millions; and the huge regions south of the Sahara in which about 160 million Negroes live. Arab Africa is almost entirely Moslem, and great sections of Negro Africa extending to almost the equatorial regions in the heart of the continent have also embraced the Moslem faith.

The people of Africa, especially those south of the Sahara, are being hurried from a tribal or feudal age into an age of nationalism and modern technology. Africa seems destined for decades of political and social upheaval. The technical assistance which the Eastern and Western blocs will inevitably pour into Africa as part of the Cold-War maneuvering will undoubtedly speed up economic and social transformation, but it may also greatly aggravate political tensions and endanger newly-won political freedom.

The largest independent Negro nation, and the most advanced of the new African states, in Nigeria. Nigeria had been the model British colony in Africa, and today it shows every sign of having the political maturity and the trained leadership to become an important member of the family of nations. Perhaps the most representative of the leaders of this new nation is Sir Abubakar Tafawa Balawa, federal Prime Minister of Nigeria.

Abubakar is dedicated to maintaining his nation's independence, but he is also a friend and admirer of Great Britain and of the British Commonwealth of Nations. He has said that the British colonial system was the best in Africa and he acknowledges the great contributions Britain has made in developing Nigeria. Though a devout Moslem, he has frequently applauded the work of the Christian missionaries in training a large part of Nigeria's educated class.

Abubakar is probably the most moderate of the new African national leaders. "Sometimes," he has said, "we have been impatient in our march toward national freedom and sometimes we criticize Britain for being overcautious, but in the long run, as events in the Congo have proved, our preparedness for the future will stand us in good stead." His pro-British and pro-Western viewpoint is accentuated by the cultured English that he speaks. A graduate of the University of London, Abubaker is one of a number of prominent Nigerian political figures who have been knighted by Queen Elizabeth.

Although Abubakar envisions that his nation will play an increasingly important role in African affairs, he is farsighted enough to acknowledge the gigantic problems his nation faces.

Nigeria has a population of about 35 million people, almost all of whom are Negro. It is a large country, about one-eighth the size of the United States, and is endowed with rich agricultural lands and mineral resources. Nigeria is one of the world's leading exporters of cocoa, vegetable oils and tin. All of the country is extremely hot, but there are great varieties of climate and geography. The coastal plains are swampy and tropical and much of the southern part consists of rainy jungles. The inland and northern regions, however, consist of rolling prairie lands and flat deserts with little rain.

Nigeria, located on the west coast of Africa, has had contact with Europe for over 400 years, and a higher percentage of its people have been trained in Western science and technology than in any other comparable African state. Nigeria is also the ancestral homeland of perhaps a majority of the Negro citizens of the United States.

In spite of its many economic and educational advances, Nigeria, like many other parts of Africa, is sharply divided along linguistic and religious lines. There is no common Nigerian language; the educated class uses English as the lingua franca. Hundreds of different languages and dialects are spoken throughout the country. There are three main language groups living in distinct parts of the country. These three groups make up about 50 per cent of the population. Each of them, along with many smaller language groups, has strong separatist feelings and wishes to keep its own political and cultural identity. For this reason, Nigeria has been formed as a federation, made up of three semi-independent regions. Each region has its own premier and its own parliament and government. The city of Lagos on the coast is the site of the federal government and is outside the three regions, with a legal status similar to that of our national capital.

The northern region has about half of Nigeria's population and more than three quarters of its territory. It is overwhelmingly Moslem. The largest and dominant language group in the north is the Hausa people, who live and work as poor farmers and herdsmen. Although the most numerous of the Nigerian peoples, they have also been the most isolated and backward, although the educational gap between this region and the other two has been greatly narrowed in recent years.

The most advanced part of Nigeria is the eastern region which stretches from the southern banks of the Niger River to the Gulf of Guinea. This is a rich, densely populated tropical region, which for hundreds of years has been a commercial and maritime center. The Ibo people form the dominant language group in the eastern region and have a reputation for being skilled traders and artisans. They are also probably the most Westernized and best educated of Nigeria's people. For over a hundred years missionary societies have operated schools and clinics in this region, and there is today a sizable Christian minority in the native population.

The western region, also bordering the Gulf of Guinea, is the richest of Nigeria's three regions. It is one of the world's main suppliers of cocoa, and it has much rubber, timber and palm oil. Many of its people live as farmers in tribal groups and are governed by an old, established aristocracy. The dominant language group here is the Yoruba.

By the year 1900 the British had established themselves as masters of Nigeria. For several hundred years before this time, however, the European powers were interested in the area. In the 18th and 19th centuries Nigeria was a main source for slaves and also for palm oil. Over the period 1914-1960 Nigeria was a colony of Great Britain. The British governed the country benevolently and followed a policy of using the local chieftains and other hereditary leaders to administer directly to the people. Although they attempted to abolish slavery and other cruel practices, the British tried not to interfere with cultural or economic life. The hot climate made Nigeria unattractive to Europeans, and the British further discouraged European settlement, limiting land ownership to the African population. This policy was intended to protect the Africans from being exploited by better educated Europeans.

After World War I, nationalist sentiment rapidly developed among the growing number of educated Nigerians. The British, slowly at first, began to allow Nigerians to take responsible positions in the colonial administation. The British Labor government that came to power in 1945 decided to grant independence to a number of overseas possessions, including India and Nigeria. These new states were to be directed into the British Commonwealth. Were it not for its sharp divisions and political animosities, Nigeria would have received its freedom in 1948 at the same time that India did. Because of intense Nigerian opposition, however, and the danger of civil war, the British delayed this grant of independence for over a decade.

In 1946 the British created the first national parliament for Nigeria and also organized embryonic governments in the three regions. In 1954, concluding that federalism was the best political arrangement for Nigeria, the British helped establish three regional governments loosely connected to the national government. Finally, in 1957, under its first federal prime minister, Abubakar, the leader of the northern region, the Federation of Nigeria became a reality.

Abubakar was born in 1912, the son of a poor butcher in the northern Hausa part of Nigeria. As a child he showed unusual brilliance and largely through self-education he was able to qualify for the only high school in the northern region. He then went to Britain and was graduated from the University of London as a teacher.

In 1947, Abubakar left teaching and entered politics. He quickly become the leading figure in the Northern People's Congress Party, which represented mainly the Moslem north. Until 1955, he actively opposed independence. He did not believe Nigeria was ready for it, and he feared that the more advanced Ibo and Yoruba peoples to the South would dominate the backward North. On several occasions he threatened a holy war if the British withdrew. In 1955, after a visit to the United States where he saw people of many different backgrounds working together, Abubakar changed his viewpoint and spoke out for independence.

In 1958, the British government under Harold Macmillan became satisfied that Nigeria was ready for freedom. It promised that if the Nigerian government to be elected in December, 1959 voted for independence, this would be granted on October 1, 1960. The 1959 election campaign was carried on with great vigor and enthusiasm by Nigeria's three major political parties which represent primarily the three regions. Abubakar's Northern People's Congress Party won more votes than either of the other two parties and it formed a coalition with the party representing mainly the eastern region, the National Council of Nigeria and the Cameroons. Abubakar, as leader of the coalition, was again chosen federal prime minister.

In January, 1960, Harold Macmillan made the first visit of a British prime minister to Nigeria. After his address to the Parliament, a unanimous resolution was passed requesting independence and Commonwealth status for Nigeria. Macmillan, who toured

Lagos, the federal capital, and a number of schools and industries in other parts of the country, was warmly received by the Nigerian people. Macmillan has been a firm supporter of the principle of freedom for the African people, and during his visit, he pledged Britain to even closer support of her new fellow member in the Commonwealth.

Symbolic loyalty to the Queen is the tie that binds Commonwealth nations; a member may break this tie at any time that it chooses. Nations such as Nigeria or India remain in the Commonwealth because they feel that membership gives them economic and political advantages; yet, it also often reflects an admiration among the educated class for the British way of life and the British political system. Certainly the veneration of the Queen and the monarchical system are strong traditions in Nigeria. Elizabeth is Queen of independent Nigeria as she is of Australia or Canada. She is represented by a governor-general, who will be the figurative head of state in her absence. It is curious that in republican India respect for the Queen and English values has grown considerably among intellectuals since the British withdrawal in 1948. Nigeria shows every sign of following India's example in this regard.

If rising young Africa is looking for a symbol, it could hardly do better than to consider the achievements of one who led his country toward independence while avoiding the pitfalls of revolutionary violence — Abubakar of Nigeria.

XII CARDENAS: BUILDER OF MODERN MEXICO

This century has witnessed a growing number of under-developed nations in Asia, Africa, and Latin America, some old, others new, aspiring to become modern states. Despite great handicaps, they are trying to overcome the illiteracy and poverty of their people; and in order to achieve some measure of economic and political equality among their citizens, they are breaking down many of the historic differences that have existed between social classes, especially between the very rich and the very poor. This transformation is being sparked by the feeling of nationalism which is influencing growing numbers of people in these countries. Nationalism is closely connected, not only with the drive for greater equality, but also with the intense desire of these people to be looked upon as equals by the advanced nations of the world.

Our neighbor to the south, Mexico, was the first of the major Latin American states to attempt a real social and political transformation of the country. Mexico's experiences may be taken as a valuable guide in understanding the situation among the many nations of the world which are still underdeveloped.

Lazaro Cardenas is the outstanding symbol of Mexico's progress. He ranks with Benito Juarez, the great Mexican-Indian patriot of the mid-19th century, as one of the most important and best loved leaders of his people. In his outlook and actions there are many startling similarities to Mahatma Gandhi of India. Both men have had a great love for the common people and for the simple life, and both tried to glorify the virtues and raise the status of the underprivileged classes.

Becoming president in 1934 at the age of 39, Cardenas made fundamental changes in Mexico's political and social structure, and set his country on its present course of development. Under him, Mexico's working and peasant classes were given a large share of participation in the government and their economic condition was improved appreciably.

By creating a firm political foundation and by his humane and moderate policies, Cardenas ended the long period of political assassinations, military revolts and dictatorships which had marked Mexico's history. Cardenas also did much to raise the international prestige of Mexico and to establish good relations, based on equality, with the United States. Although he has remained largely out of politics since his retirement as president in 1940, he is still a major influence for peace and stability in Mexico. Perhaps his greatest contribution was the peaceful transfer of power from one president to the next, a process which he inaugurated, and which has been an important factor underlying Mexico's progress.

Mexico is a nation of over 30 million people. Despite the rapid growth of cities, most of her population is made up of poor farmers. Most Mexicans are of mixed Spanish and Indian blood, but there are also many pure-blooded Indians. Although Cardenas and his successors did much to raise the status of the lower classes, there are still great contrasts in Mexican society. Much of the peasantry lives under primitive conditions, drawing from the soil a meager and substandard livelihood. The diet consists of few staples, corn, often in the form of tortillas, being the most common.

Illiteracy is still prevalent, especially among the more backward Indians, although rural schools are growing in number. Because of the limited amount of good farmland, one of Mexico's most serious problems has been her increasing surplus of farm labor—especially in view of the fact that Mexico's birth rate is one of the world's highest.

In recent years, encouraged by the economic boom of World War II and by American investments and tourism, a sizable middle class, although small by U.S. standards, has grown up.

Composed of teachers and other professionals, small businessmen, and the huge governmental bureaucracy, this middle class, concentrated in the cities, is now a major force in Mexican politics.

There remains an influential, but numerically small, upper

class, composed of the newly rich and long-established families of Spanish descent. In spite of the increased feeling of national unity which Cardenas and others have promoted, there is still a wide gulf between these classes.

The turning point in modern Mexican history occurred in 1910, when the aged military dictator Porfirio Diaz was overthrown by a revolt, the leader of which sought to give the country a more liberal and democratic government. Although the rebellion was enthusiastically supported by the mass of the people, especially the peasantry and the new industrial working class, most of its leaders were generals or rich provincial landowners. For over a decade, Mexico was engaged in civil war, with rival generals competing for authority, and central government weak or nonexistent.

A new constitution was promulgated in 1917, which advanced the basic ideas of the revolution, and which is still in force today. This constitution has four main points: first, that the soil and the mineral wealth of Mexico belong to its people; second, that labor has the right to organize and to bargain collectively; third, that the political power of the church in Mexico should be limited; and fourth, that the great landed estates of the country should be divided among the peasants.

In 1924, a powerful general, Plutarço Calles, made himself president, established some order in the country, and controlled Mexican politics until 1934, when Cardenas assumed office as president.

Cardenas was born in 1895 of a poor family. After receiving a primary school education, he went to work as a bookkeeper. While very young, he joined the anti-Diaz revolutionary movement, and by the age of 18, he became a professional soldier. He served under the leading generals in the civil war period and was fortunate enough to have been on the winning side. By the age of 25, he had become a Brigadier General and aligned himself with Calles, becoming one of the latter's key aides. Under Calles, Cardenas became governor of one of the Mexican states and in 1929, was appointed first president of the new National Revolutionary Party. Since this time, this party, under various names, has dominated Mexican politics. In 1934, at Calles' direction, the party nominated Cardenas for the presidency of Mexico. By then Cardenas had already exhibited his integrity and had succeeded in identifying himself with the common people. Calles and his clique, however, were misled by Cardenas' quiet nature and fastidious concern for detail into believing that he was weak and could be controlled by them. In spite of the fact that the support of the National Revolutionary Party already assured his election, Cardenas campaigned extensively over all of Mexico, visiting hundreds of villages and factories—hoping thereby to gain a broad base of popular support.

Cardenas, on becoming president, immediately set out to break the power of Calles—once his mentor, but now a political rival. In a period of a year, he had gradually but systematically removed all Calles' supporters from the government and the army. In 1935, fully in control, Cardenas arranged a plane flight to take Calles into exile in California.

Although Cardenas strengthened his government in some areas, and gave a psychological boost to the morale of the Mexican people, he has nevertheless been rightly criticized for having been an inefficient administrator. He consumed much of his time traveling about from village to village listening to the grievances of the common people and hearing scores of petitioners on petty matters in his office. Many of his most important aides, in the Mexican political tradition, were somewhat corrupt and incompetent. Cardenas tried to take care of too many details by himself, neglecting the more important policy directives. However, his sincere concern for the Mexican people won him their loyalty and devotion, and gave him the political strength to carry out his sweeping social reforms.

The great support which Cardenas engendered was transferred to the National Revolutionary Party. In 1938, being firmly established as the leader of Mexico, Cardenas rebuilt the NRP, changing its name to the Mexican Revolutionary Party. He built the party on the three segments of the population that were firmly committed to his programs: the peasants, the trade unions, and the army. Candidates for any political office in Mexico were to be chosen from one of these three elements, and once the candidate was chosen, the entire party was to pledge its support. Although the Mexican Revolutionary Party has local chapters, and youth and women's groups throughout Mexico, it is basically an electoral organization, much like our Democratic or Republican Parties. It has never been a totalitarian party, since it does not aim at capturing the whole society of the country.

Since Cardenas' administration, the party has become increasingly bureaucratized, and has lost much of the idealism it had under Cardenas. Nevertheless, it remains the dominant and guiding force in Mexican political life. Several opposition parties have arisen which have criticized the reforms of the 1917 constitution, but these have not yet become a major political force. Since the Mexican Revolutionary Party conducts the elections and counts the ballots, such political changes as may occur in the future will most likely have to come from within the Revolutionary Party rather than from the outside.

Cardenas was less an innovator than an implementer of policy. He carried out the revolutionary provisions of the 1917 constitution, which, except with regard to its restrictions on the church, had not been fulfilled by his predecessors. Cardenas had no systematic policy objectives, other than to put an end to the exploitation of Mexican agricultural and industrial workers, and to eliminate the more ruthless forms of exploitation of Mexican natural resources by foreigners.

Mexico's oldest and most glaring social problem was that of land ownership. Prior to Cardenas' administration, much of Mexico's good farmland was part of the huge plantations that were owned by a handful of rich families. The peasants, or *peones*, were little more than serfs on these quasi-feudal estates. Even in 1910 the problem of equitable land distribution had reached acute proportions, and the situation was well understood by the revolutionaries who wrote the 1917 constitution; but until Cardenas, the revolutionary leaders were not strong enough or interested enough to alter it appreciably. Cardenas therefore proceeded to break up the landed estates rapidly, dividing them either into peasant cooperatives or into individual small farms, and paying compensation to the former owners. He organized the powerful National Peasants' Confederation on a local and national level, and mde it one of the three controlling bodies within the revolutionary party.

The peasants' confederation included a rural militia, which was a necessary tool to insure the success of this agrarian policy. Cardenas also set up improved credit facilities, and training farms and experimental stations to raise farming standards. Mexico is still beset by serious agricultural problems; there remains a great surplus of farm labor, and farming methods and equipment are poor. However, as a consequence of Cardenas' efforts, the old feudalistic plantation system is gone forever.

Mexico's growing and radical industrial working class also achieved power as a result of Cardenas' efforts and support. Laws were passed favoring workers in their relationship with management and encouraging the growth and responsibility of trade unions. In 1936, under Cardenas' guidance, the Mexican Workers' Confederation was organized—the second major pillar of Mexico's government—and it came to represent most of the organized Mexican workers. A governmental board of arbitrators was used to resolve strikes between labor and management, and under Cardenas, the board's decision usually favored labor. Foreign businessmen especially felt that they were being discriminated against by the board, and by Cardenas' policies in general.

Mexican nationalists had long looked with suspicion and envy at the great foreign companies that extracted mineral wealth from their homelands. These companies have often been the nationalists' immediate target. For several years, the newly-formed oil workers' union and the oil companies had been engaged in a bitter dispute. The board of arbitrators finally investigated the situation, and reported in 1938 that the oil companies' profits were excessive, and that the workers' demands, in effect, were fair. The oil companies reluctantly accepted the substance of the recommendation, but demanded that Cardenas agree in writing to the compromise terms of the settlement. This provoked Cardenas, and he proceeded to nationalize Mexico's oil industry.

Many observers feel that Cardenas' views and policies have hurt Mexico's economic development by excessively badgering and restricting business interests, especially foreign. In the long run, however, by raising the prestige and political influence of the trade unions, he greatly advanced the cause of democracy and peaceful progress in Mexico. The huge trade union organs in

Mexico today, monuments to Cardenas, remain powerful in the government but have lost much of their early idealism. Even though they are today huge bureaucracies intermeshed in the general leadership of the government and badly in need of reform, they still represent a major advance for Mexican labor.

Most of the revolutionary leaders in Mexico, including Cardenas, were in the liberal tradition and strongly anti-church. They sought to weaken ecclesiastical influence and control in politics and frequently persecuted church officials and religious orders. However, because of the deep religious sentiments of most Mexicans, especially the peasants, and because he wanted to reduce the bitter hatred and strife which divided Mexico, Cardenas in 1936 ended the harassment of the church and made friendly overtures to its leaders. Many of them, in turn, quickly began to give support to Cardenas and his government. Anti-clericalism in Mexico has greatly diminished as an issue of importance since 1936.

Cardenas has been called a socialist and a communist by many of his domestic and foreign critics. While president, it is true that he described himself as a socialist, frequently used socialistic slogans, and had a number of known Communists in high positions. Still, Cardenas was not committed to a program of nationalization of Mexico's industry and property. What did appeal to him in socialism was its humanitarianism and its emphasis on equality. Although he occasionally hailed the economic achievements of the Soviet Union, he was a consistent critic of the dictatorship there and of the Soviet's denial of basic human rights. Since the beginning of the Cold War, he has sharply condemned Soviet expansionism and its enslavement of other nations.

In many underdeveloped countries, nationalist leaders such as Cardenas have advocated some degree of governmental ownership of industry and natural wealth as essential to their nations' progress. Frequently, we Americans, with our highly productive capitalistic system, are suspicious of such men, and regard them as the unwitting dupes of our great Cold-War enemy, the socialist Soviet Union. In reality, such leaders are often our best allies in resisting Soviet imperialism. In nations such as Mexico where business leaders often lack a sense of responsibility, and where the propertied classes have little inclination to invest in long-range industrialization, nationalization may be the best and only way to advance the country's economy. We may disagree with such leaders and with the great numbers of intellectuals, especially students, in these countries who sympathize with socialism, but we jeopardize our own security and the cause of human freedom by dogmatically opposing them. Our main concern should be whether or not they are subordinating their own national interests to those of the Soviet Union.

Cardenas was an early supporter of Roosevelt's Good Neighbor policy toward Latin America. Although Cardenas frequently criticized private U.S. business interests and American policies in support of them, he was a strong advocate of U.S.-Mexican friendship. This was well illustrated in 1939, when he pledged Mexican support to the United States if we went to war.

Cardenas retired at the end of his term in 1940, and facilitated the peaceful accession of the next president. When the United States went to war in 1941, he actively supported Mexico's entry into the war on the Allied side, and he accepted the position of minister of war in Mexico's wartime government. Cardenas' successors as president have also been friendly toward the United States and have, to a greater extent than he, encouraged private American investments.

The basic principles of the Mexican Revolution, which Cardenas began to carry out, still motivate Mexico's leaders, including the current president, Adolfo Lopez Mateos. Many observers believe that if Mexico is to progress more rapidly she must revive the sense of justice and freedom that characterized her revolution. Certainly the example of Mexico's greatest living political figure, Lazaro Cardenas, may yet inspire her people to rise and meet this challenge.

PHOTO CREDITS